Advance praise for The Pedagogy of Teacher Activism

"These intricate, irresistible sketches of teachers teaching illuminate the dynamism, complexity, and practical ethics on display daily in hundreds of thousands of public school classrooms. Keith Catone, the teaching artist drawing these portraits, is not alone—each of his subjects is also an active collaborator who comes to life in school as a three-dimensional human being, trembling, approachable, vibrant, and real. We watch these teachers struggling to teach free people for full participation in a democracy in spite of a system that denies them—teachers and students alike—agency and recognition at every turn. We begin to experience teaching for social justice and teacher activism not as the precious province of a distinct or specialized group of people, nor as an add-on to everyday teaching, but rather as a practice inextricably linked to ordinary good work. Here is a pedagogy that foregrounds the arts of liberty—imagination, initiative, courage, curiosity, open investigation—toward the creation of a future fit for all children, a place of joy and justice powered by love."

—William Ayers, Distinguished Professor of Education and Senior University Scholar, the University of Illinois at Chicago (retired); Author of _To Teach, Fugitive Days,_ and _Demand the Impossible! A Radical Manifesto_

"Against simplistic and caricatured images of 'teacher' and 'activist' that pervade public discourse come Keith Catone's timely and inspiring portraits that bring great nuance to the intersection of teacher-activist. For current and aspiring teachers and teacher educators, _The Pedagogy of Teacher Activism_ richly reveals how teaching is transformative precisely as it manifests critical consciousness and community activism. Read this book and reignite your passion to teach towards social justice."

—Kevin Kumashiro, Dean, University of San Francisco School of Education; Author of _Bad Teacher!: How Blaming Teachers Distorts the Bigger Picture_

"In our popular views and cultural imagery we rarely picture teachers as activists, with voice and agency, with political and ethical commitments that shape their lives both inside and outside the classroom. More often we envision teachers as passive, muted, unimaginative bystanders whose role and power are strictly circumscribed by school policies and bureaucracies. In his insightful and provocative book, Keith Catone offers a counternarrative, composing rich portraits of four teachers with voice and vision, intellect and imagination, who courageously challenge the injustices and inequalities that pervade the structure, culture, curriculum, and pedagogies of the schools they inhabit and the communities they seek to change."

—Sara Lawrence-Lightfoot, Emily Hargroves Fisher Professor of Education at Harvard University; Author of _The Good High School, The Essential Conversation,_ and _Respect_

The Pedagogy of
Teacher Activism

Narrative, Dialogue, and the Political Production of Meaning

Michael Peters & Peter McLaren
Series Editors

Vol. 11

The Education and Struggle series is part of the Peter Lang Education list.
Every volume is peer reviewed and meets
the highest quality standards for content and production.

PETER LANG
New York • Bern • Frankfurt • Berlin
Brussels • Vienna • Oxford • Warsaw

Keith C. Catone

The Pedagogy of Teacher Activism

Portraits of Four Teachers for Justice

PETER LANG
New York • Bern • Frankfurt • Berlin
Brussels • Vienna • Oxford • Warsaw

Library of Congress Cataloging-in-Publication Data

Names: Catone, Keith, author.
Title: The pedagogy of teacher activism:
portraits of four teachers for justice / Keith C. Catone.
Description: New York: Peter Lang, 2016.
Series: Education and struggle: narrative, dialogue
and the political production of meaning; vol. 11
ISSN 2168-6432 (print) | ISSN 2168-6459 (online)
Includes bibliographical references.
Identifiers: LCCN 2016039567 | ISBN 978-1-4331-3437-1 (hardcover: alk. paper)
ISBN 978-1-4331-3436-4 (paperback: alk. paper) | ISBN 978-1-4539-1916-3 (ebook pdf)
ISBN 978-1-4331-3868-3 (epub) | ISBN 978-1-4331-3869-0 (mobi)
Subjects: LCSH: Teachers—Political activity—United States—Case studies.
Social justice—Study and teaching—United States—Case studies.
Classification: LCC LB2844.1.P6 C38 2017 | DDC 371.1—dc23
DOI: 10.3726/b10573
LC record available at https://lccn.loc.gov/2016039567

Bibliographic information published by **Die Deutsche Nationalbibliothek**.
Die Deutsche Nationalbibliothek lists this publication in the "Deutsche
Nationalbibliografie"; detailed bibliographic data are available
on the Internet at http://dnb.d-nb.de/.

The paper in this book meets the guidelines for permanence and durability
of the Committee on Production Guidelines for Book Longevity
of the Council of Library Resources.

Printed in the United States of America

Dedicated to the inspiring work of committed teacher activists throughout the world who are engaged in the beautiful struggle for justice, to the young people, families, and communities who motivate me to continue to fight for a better world, to the New York Collective of Radical Educators and the entire national network of Teacher Activist Groups who have nurtured me and many others along our paths forging purpose, power, and possibility, and to my son, Ishaan, who I hope will be taught by teachers as dedicated to changing the world as the four whose stories fill these pages.

TABLE OF CONTENTS

FOREWORD

Leigh Patel

American society is replete with chasms between word and deed. The land of freedom incarcerates exponentially more than any other nation on the planet, continues to break records deporting vulnerabilized populations, and engages in myriad legal and extralegal violence upon minoritized populations. Despite its constant avowal of being a site for freedom, democracy, and opportunity, U.S. practices domestically and internationally are marked more by the logics and longstanding history of racist capitalism (Gilmore, 2007; Robinson, 1983). Unsurprisingly, this contradiction is fully embodied in the field of education. In the imaginary, education is the single most sure pathway to upward social mobility, yet in reality it is society's most efficient conduit for stratification and disciplining of social acceptability.

The four teacher activists you will meet in the pages of this book share a vital theoretical orientation in common: they refuse to participate in the widespread fantasy that the chasm between word and deed does not exist. Even more radically, they refuse to concede that such stark contrasts between mission and practice are intractable. Keith Catone provides beautifully descriptive and caringly contextualized etchings of how these four women came to be agents for change, who refuse that education merely be a site of social reproduction. Catone connects to and extends upon a vital component of this refusal—the apprehension, the temporary suspension of dynamic forces so that these dynamic forces may be altered. Put more simply, it is difficult to alter what you cannot see or hear. Catone guides the reader to follow the pastiche histories of four activist teachers who apprehended societal harm and reconfigured their personal professional lives to effect change.

Like the women whose portraits he illuminates, Catone makes a key move of refusal. He refuses to concede that pedagogy be conflated with teaching technique. He disallows the reader from projecting the still-dominant education trope of "how to." There is no lesson plan here, no rubric for evaluating the activism-icity of teachers. Thank goodness. Instead, the details are equally vivid and varied, reflecting the nature of how they are lived. Catone upholds an elusive and vitally needed "conceptual orientation," as he terms it, to lived pedagogy: there is no singular way. The method is in the multiplicity. It cannot be reduced to a replicable series of steps. And furthermore, it is never personless. Best practices, a harmful yet consistent trope in education, conjures mythic objectivity. Practices are always specific: taken up by specific people acting within specific contexts. In these portraits, woven by Catone and his concise, sharp commentary, it becomes more and more impossible to contend that anyone could merely follow the same biographic steps and emerge as a teacher activist. In these details and descriptions, Catone disallows education from furthering the fallacy that pedagogy, let alone cultural transformation, is mere logarithm.

Of course, refusal has its entire and still incomplete history in populations who were never meant to profit from the heteropatriarchal white settler colonial structure of the United States. Audra Simpson's (2007) foundational work on indigenous refusal theorizes how freedom-seeking as an act of refusal is fundamentally a praxis of sovereignty. Gloria Anzaldúa, an important theorist in Catone's work, conceptualized (2012) the borderlands not because she viewed herself as a border crosser incarnate but because her knowledge from the margins could apprehend the dialectic between the constructed center and margins in ways that dominant worldviews simply could not.

As I read about these four dynamic teacher activists and immersed myself in Catone's careful annotation and analysis, I was reminded of Anna Julia Cooper. Cooper, one of the most prominent Black theorists in American history, was an activist and educator throughout her life. Her work consistently attended to both societal structure and structures of education. In 1892, Cooper (1988), in the still relevant book, *A Voice from the South*, posited that the nation as a whole would benefit from the more comprehensive social uplift and educational advancement of Black people, particularly Black women. Offering an astute appraisal of the impactful yet not determinant role of socialization, Cooper theorized that a more pervasive and empowered presence of women would bring more intellectual elegance to education, balancing the competitive and individualist ways that men are condoned to act in society. While none of these socialized roles are static, Cooper, and the teacher activists whom you will learn about from Catone's elegant description and analysis, speak confidently through words and actions of the beautiful, undeniable entanglements of beings, learning, and society.

Throughout, and in the end, this book raises important questions about what it means to regard education and pedagogy as always constitutive of society. This book was researched and written during an era when minimally "trained" teachers can leapfrog into educational politics and then municipal politics on the mantle of having been in the trenches. This profiting from a few years' dabbling in teaching can only be possible when there is widespread simplification of the complexity and intertwined nature of schooling and society. This book offers an important, and much needed alternative to educational research that describes the symptom reduction du jour. The four women in this book and Catone's expert guidance remind us that by contending with how formal education contributes to societal ills, we are much better positioned to alter those conditions.

References

Anzaldúa, G. (2012). *Borderlands/la frontera: The new Mestiza* (4th ed.). San Francisco: Aunt Lute Books.

Cooper, A. J. (1988). *A voice from the south*. New York: Oxford University Press.

Gilmore, R. W. (2007). *Golden gulag: Prisons, surplus, crisis, and opposition in globalizing California*. Berkeley, CA: University of California Press.

Robinson, C. J. (1983). *Black Marxism: The making of the black radical tradition*. Chapel Hill, NC: University of North Carolina Press.

Simpson, A. (2007). On ethnographic refusal: Indigeneity, 'voice' and colonial citizenship. *Junctures: The Journal for Thematic Dialogue, 9*, 67–80.

ACKNOWLEDGMENTS

This book has been made possible by the love and support of so many. First, I am forever indebted to Rosie Frascella, Lisa North, Kari Kokka, and Natalia Ortiz for opening up their classrooms, lives, and memories to my prying inquiries. The journey they each took with me over the past few years has been long and steady. I am thankful for their perseverance. Further, my good friend, former teacher, and artist, Rudy Bravo has blessed the cover with original painted portraits of each woman who appears in this book. Thank you.

My first students and teaching community at Banana Kelly High School in the South Bronx have been a source of inspiration for everything I have done and accomplished in my career. My doctoral committee members, Mark Warren, Sara Lawrence-Lightfoot, and William Ayers, were each instrumental in helping me see this project through from start to finish. I am especially indebted to Dr. Ayers, who never stopped asking me when my book was going to be ready. Dr. Karen Mapp has always been a present, steady source of support.

I have a supportive community of coconspirators. The New York Collective of Radical Educators (NYCoRE) continue to be a source of inspiration. A special shout out goes to Bree Picower, whose scholarship on grassroots teacher activism has laid much of the groundwork for works like mine. Thank you to the Annenberg Institute for School Reform at Brown University, and especially to Warren Simmons, Mike Grady, Richard Gray, and Alexa LeBoeuf, for providing me the space and opportunity to integrate writing into my work. My close friends and incredible writing group, Carla Shalaby and Thomas Nikundiwe, attended to my work with diligent care and attention. Leigh Patel not only graced these pages with her beautiful foreword but also shared invaluable critique that only made my work stronger.

I have always relied on the support of my family. During data collection trips, I stayed with my grandmother (Ahma), Elaine Coleman, who always made sure that I had food in my belly. My in-laws, Pronoti and Umesh Tahbildar, always offered their excited support. My parents, Debbie and Bill Catone, never stopped showing genuine interest and pride in my work.

Most importantly, many thanks to my life partner, Dulari Tahbildar, who vowed, when we married, to walk next to me in the struggle for justice. Whatever part of the struggle this book represents, the steadfast and unfailing commitment we have made to loving each other and nurturing a family together is the stuff that true purpose, power, and possibility are made of.

LIST OF ABBREVIATIONS

AFT—American Federation of Teachers
AP—Advanced Placement
CEC—Community Education Council
CEJ—Coalition for Educational Justice
CORE—Caucus of Rank-and-File Educators
CTU—Chicago Teachers Union
CUNY—City University of New York
DA—Delegate Assembly
DOE—Department of Education
ESL—English as a Second Language
FMPR—Federacion de Maestros de Puerto Rico
GEM—Grassroots Education Movement
GLSEN—Gay, Lesbian, and Straight Education Network
GMHC—Gay Men's Health Crisis
GSA—Gay-Straight Alliance
IHSPS—International High School at Prospect Heights
ItAG—Inquiry to Action Group
JREC—Julia Richman Education Complex
LES—Lower East Side

LGBTQ—Lesbian, Gay, Bisexual, Transgender, Queer
MORE—Movement of Rank-and-File Educators
MTEA—Milwaukee Teachers Education Association
NEA—National Education Association
NYCoRE—New York Collective of Radical Educators
PBA—Performance-Based Assessment
PD—Professional Development
PEP—Panel for Education Policy
PTA—Parent Teacher Association
REACH—Representing Education Activism and Community through
          Hip-Hop
SEIU—Service Employees International Union
SNCC—Student Nonviolent Coordinating Committee
TAG—Teacher Activist Groups
TDU—Teamsters for a Democratic Union
TU—Teachers Unite
UAW—United Auto Workers
UFT—United Federation of Teachers
VB—Venceremos Brigade
WBCHS—West Brooklyn Community High School
YLB—Youth Leadership Board

INTRODUCTION: (IN)SIGHTING TEACHER ACTIVISM

In December 2008, after President-elect Barack Obama nominated Arne Duncan, Superintendent of Chicago Public Schools, as U.S. Secretary of Education, Duncan released a statement proclaiming that "education is the civil rights issue of our generation." He is not the only one to have invoked the U.S. Civil Rights Movement when talking about the issue of education and he certainly will not be the last. However, Secretary Duncan's consistent framing of education as the civil rights issue of our time along with the federal government's championing of education reform policies served to place the issue of education on the front burner of U.S. consciousness for the better part of the early 21st century.

> This little school of mine, we're gonna let it shine.
> This little school of mine, we're gonna let it shine.
> This little school of mine, we're gonna let it shine.
> Let it shine, let it shine, let it shine.

In January 2011, I attended a New York City (NYC) Department of Education (DOE) Panel for Education Policy (PEP) meeting. Among those present, one was a teacher activist named Lisa North. Lisa was a veteran elementary school teacher in Brooklyn with 20 years of experience. She started teaching only after her son was born and she decided not to go back to her job as an Entenmann's delivery truck driver, a union job she had taken after leaving college to be more involved in labor rights activism. Growing up as a White child in rural Maryland, Lisa was too young to be involved in the Civil Rights Movement, but attended the University of Michigan in Ann Arbor in the mid-1970s and immersed herself in leftist politics, which exposed her to antiwar, women's rights, gay rights, and labor activism. When she was a young girl wishing she could be more involved in the Civil Rights Movement, it was Lisa's parents who told her that there would be plenty of struggles for her to engage in when she grew older. Nearly 50 years later at the PEP meeting, Lisa joined teacher, student, and other education activists in belting out a new rendition of the children's gospel song "This Little Light of Mine," intentionally invoking the Civil Rights Movement. Including Lisa, at least thirty Grassroots Education Movement (GEM) teacher activists were responsible for passing out the song lyrics on homemade fliers to protest what had become the DOE's annual practice of closing schools throughout the city.

This little school of mine, we're not gonna let it close, no.
This little school of mine, we're not gonna let it close, no.
This little school of mine, we're not gonna let it close, no.
We love our teacher, we love our school and it shows.

Many were also there to demonstrate against the recent appointment of Cathie Black as NYC Schools Chancellor as she presided over her first PEP meeting. Just months earlier, the previous NYC Schools Chancellor Joel Klein had announced his resignation and Mayor Michael Bloomberg appointed Black, a magazine and media executive, to succeed him. Black's appointment caused a whirlwind of controversy given that she had held no prior public administration positions and lacked any related education credentials. Her appointment seemed a hyperbolic manifestation of a broader trend of appointing urban district superintendents who did not have professional backgrounds in the field of education. Ultimately, the backlash against Chancellor Black became so great that Mayor Bloomberg was forced to replace her in April 2011, just after three months.

All around the school, we're more than just test scores, oh.
All around the school, we're more than just test scores, oh.
All around the school, we're more than just test scores, oh.
Cathie Black, take a step back, learn some more.

Whether people imagine ranting ideologues at the front of classrooms who forcefully indoctrinate students with leftist rhetoric or rowdy crowds of teachers at protest rallies screaming their grievances through bullhorns or, more recently, prolific Twitter users sending out forceful and strident messages of protest and resistance 140 characters at a time, I have found that our collective imagination has a hard time moving beyond these superficial (at best) and stereotypical (at worst) notions of what it means to be a teacher activist. However, when I stood and sang alongside those gathered at the PEP meeting, I glanced over at Lisa and thought of the many conversations we had about her teaching and activism. I knew that just seeing this protest, while powerful and moving, hardly scratched the surface of what it really meant for her to be there.

This is a book about four teachers—Rosie Frascella, Natalia Ortiz, Kari Kokka, and Lisa North—who believe that as teachers they are change agents, and who link their teacher roles to social justice activism. To be clear, this is not a book about how to be a teacher activist. Rather, it is a book that tells the stories about how four teacher activists be(come), which help uncover important pedagogical underpinnings of teacher activism.

Why is the pedagogy of teacher activism important? The persistent work of teacher activists displays an optimistic excitement that stands out when overall measurements of teacher job satisfaction and morale are at the lowest points in a quarter century (MetLife, 2013). With dominant reform narratives positioning teachers as "bad" (Kumashiro, 2012; Simmons, 2013), the consistent dedication of teachers who work hard in and out of schools on a daily basis is something to be celebrated and recognized as "good." The more we understand about teacher activists like Rosie, Natalia, Kari, and Lisa, the more likely we will be to cultivate others to join the teacher activist ranks and the more effective we can be at supporting them in what they do. Through the pedagogy of teacher activism, educators will more likely contribute to the realization of the pressing need for equity and justice by addressing the civil, social, and human rights issues of our time.

My Journey

Before I share the portraits of Rosie, Natalia, Kari, and Lisa, it is important to understand a bit of my journey as a teacher activist. I fell in love with teaching after working with a local academic enrichment program, which I had joined in the summer after my first year of college, and as an afterschool tutor during the following school year. For me, this love affair stemmed from how much fun I had working with young people and my evolving sense of how important education is to the larger struggle for social justice in the United States. I had entered college thinking that I would major in International Relations with a focus on global inequities and supporting "developing countries." But my lens for understanding and examining inequity shifted due to my experience in teaching public middle school students from Providence, Rhode Island, and the relationships that I developed with them and their families. I grew up just 30 minutes away from Providence, in a well-resourced town, home, and school system. I knew I had advantages as a child, but did not know how much until my experience of working with young people in Providence. The social and economic challenges they faced, ranging from episodes of street violence and police harassment to their families struggling to make rent, presented obstacles that I never had to consider as a child. The resilience my students showed in the face of such adversity as opposed to my relatively comfortable childhood made me realize that while I was studying the effects and dynamics of international injustice, there were stark realities of injustice right in my backyard.

While I was enrolled in the undergraduate teacher education program at my school, I was also emerging as an activist. I was active on campus through student of color organizations, developing an analysis of oppression and institutionalized "-isms," which led to coordinated student activism challenging the university administration and community to fully address issues of racism, classism, sexism, and heterosexism. We held workshops on power and privilege, encouraging peers to examine their own privileges based on their identities and to work against the institutional inequities that result from unexamined privilege. We planned campuswide programming to celebrate the histories of communities of color in the United States. I sought to engage in activism through local community-based organizations fighting for racial and economic justice.

Most important for me, I saw my activism and my decision to become a teacher as inextricably linked. I took seriously the idea that I was, as the title of one of my favorite course texts proclaimed, "teaching to change the world" (Oakes & Lipton, 1999). I identified schools as sites for social justice struggle and also felt it natural for teachers to be involved in community activism. I saw connections between issues of social inequality as related to and reflected in public schools and saw teachers as potential agents of change. To me, this meant that teachers, especially those in urban communities, should be involved in activism.

Armed with these beliefs, I taught in New York City for five years. My years of teaching in New York were driven and defined by my development as a teacher activist. The work I did inside and outside of my classroom represented attempts to challenge injustice. Many of my actions were specific to my immediate role as a high school social studies teacher, such as resisting the high-stakes test culture of New York City high schools by designing curricula with social justice objectives or working with school leadership to institute a stronger focus on helping students to see themselves as agents of change within their communities. I was able to design "Community Building," a course that was taught to every ninth-grader entering our school and which focused on students identifying and researching social problems faced by them and by their communities.

Outside of my school, I was active primarily through the New York Collective of Radical Educators (NYCoRE), a grassroots teacher activist group that I helped form in 2002. Founded by just six teachers from two schools—mine in the South Bronx and another in Brooklyn—NYCoRE has since grown to include an email listserv that reaches thousands. When the organization was formed, NYCoRE aimed to bring teachers together to collectively address issues in our schools and communities, such as increased and misleading military recruitment efforts in post-9/11 NYC or the implementation of even more high-stakes tests across the city at the elementary level. We found that our work began to resonate with many teachers, who started to show up at our meetings, across the city. I moved away from NYC in 2005 and NYCoRE continued to grow. Today, the group organizes hundreds of educators on a yearly basis to engage in social and educational justice activism in New York City, hosts an annual conference that attracts over 1,000 participants, writes and produces curricula and teaching resources disseminated to thousands of educators across the United States, and participates as a founding member of the national network of Teacher Activist Groups (TAG).

Sighting Teacher Activists

In 2008, when I had the opportunity to research teacher activism, I found my curiosity was most piqued by seeking to understand more about why and how people be(come) teacher activists. More specifically, I sought to address the following questions with individual teacher activists who would be generous enough to work with me:

- How do these teacher activists understand and explain the development of their approaches to teaching and activism?

- How do they see their life histories informing these approaches to teaching and activism?
- From their perspectives, how do they attempt to put their teacher activist commitments into practice?
- What do they identify as the challenges they face and supports they rely upon in their work?

I decided to focus on teacher activists from New York City for three reasons. First, the NYC teacher activist context is the one that I know the best. It is where I was a teacher activist for five years and it made sense to do research in a place I knew well. Second, connections in New York City would also provide an entrée for establishing relationships with teacher activists there. Being a founding member of NYCoRE, I brought an assumed level of trust and solidarity from the start of the project, even though I knew only one of the participants previously. Finally, concentrating on one location meant I could visit frequently enough during data collection to maintain a regular presence.

I sought to engage teacher activists who were members of NYCoRE, but with whom I had not worked closely. I wanted to include teachers who were active in NYCoRE consistently for at least a year and had taken on active leadership roles, having demonstrated a commitment to teacher activism both inside and outside the classroom. I also wanted to maintain a focus on classroom teachers, not afterschool educators, community-based organization staff, or other education-related professionals, who commonly engage with NYCoRE. Finally, as much as possible, I wanted the four participants to reflect diversity in terms of personal and social identities (e.g., race, gender, sexual orientation, class background, etc.) and professional roles (e.g., teaching experience, subject area, school level, etc.).

With an eye toward the various diversity criteria listed above, NYCoRE core leaders helped identify four participants who varied in age, racial identities, sexual orientation, and class backgrounds. Three taught high school across three different subject areas and one taught early elementary. They varied in teaching experience between 4 and 18 years. They were all women, a product mostly of active NYCoRE membership, which was estimated by leaders as at least 70 percent female.

In addition to Lisa North, whom readers met in the opening scene above, three other teacher activists would open up their classrooms, memories, and lives to my prying inquiry over the course of the next three school years:

- Rosie Frascella grew up in a White, middle-class family in Hamilton, New Jersey, and by 2011 she had taught high school English and history for the past six years in both upper Manhattan and Brooklyn. She was trained as an English as a second language (ESL) teacher through the Peace Corps Fellows Program at Teachers College at Columbia University. Before becoming a teacher, Rosie was a labor union organizer and cut her activist teeth as a queer student activist in college.

- Natalia Ortiz started teaching high school history in 2006 in Brooklyn. She wanted to be a teacher when she was in elementary school, a desire that become more politicized during her college years. A native New Yorker, her father is Puerto Rican, but Natalia was raised primarily by her mother, an immigrant from Chile. She is passionate about teaching, history, and politics and is an active member of the Venceremos Brigade, a group that has organized annual trips to Cuba in open violation of the U.S. government travel restrictions since 1969.

- Kari Kokka grew up in San Jose, California, and went to a large urban public high school. She did not think about becoming a teacher until after she realized that she did not want to be an engineer after majoring in mechanical engineering at Stanford University. She became a high school math teacher and by 2011 she had taught for 10 years in New York City. She avidly practices Capoeira, an Afro-Brazilian martial art. Both of her parents' families were sent to Japanese-American internment camps during World War II, a history that is important to Kari.

In the following chapter, I first review literature that examines teachers' work as activists. Then, exploring the themes of becoming an activist and teaching to change the world, I provide readers with an analytic framework through which to view teacher activist portraits. The second chapter concludes with a description of my methodology—portraiture—which affords me a unique opportunity to explore the stories of each participant with a blend of scientific rigor and artful analysis. Each of the next four chapters presents the individual portraits of Rosie Frascella, Natalia Ortiz, Kari Kokka, and Lisa North. Then, in the final chapter I outline the pedagogy of teacher activism by drawing out lessons of purpose, power, and possibility through a cross-case analysis of the four portraits. The last chapter concludes with a statement of the overarching implications of the pedagogy of teacher activism for social justice teacher educators, teacher activist groups, and teacher unions as important players in the ongoing struggle for educational and social justice.

References

Kumashiro, K.K. (2012). *Bad teacher: How blaming teachers distorts the bigger picture.* New York: Teachers College Press.

MetLife, Inc. (2013). *The MetLife survey of the American teacher: Challenges for school leadership.* New York: MetLife Foundation. Retrieved March 23, 2013, from https://www.metlife.com/metlife-foundation/about/survey-american-teacher.html?WT.mc_id=vu1101

Oakes, J. & Lipton, M. (1999). *Teaching to change the world.* Boston: McGraw-Hill College.

Simmons, W. (2013, May 9). *What do we know about "reformers."* Speech presented at the Learning First Alliance Leadership Council Meeting. Retrieved September 20, 2013, from http://www.learningfirst.org/sites/default/files/assets/Leadership%20Council%20Meeting%202013%20Report.pdf

RESEARCHING TEACHER ACTIVISM: TRADITIONS, FRAMING, AND METHOD

Teacher Activist Traditions

There are at least three traditions of teacher activism evident in the literature: (1) feminist educator activism; (2) teacher union activism; and (3) new grassroots teacher activism. In the real lives of teacher activists—as the portraits of Rosie, Natalia, Kari, and Lisa will illustrate—these traditions can overlap with each other depending on the work in which teachers are engaged; here I will discuss them distinctly.

Feminist Educator Activism

In general, feminist activism emphasizes not only the public sphere and public political actions aimed at addressing social injustice but also the political significance of personal lives, experiences, and silenced voices of marginalized peoples (Casey, 1993; Collins, 2009; Morgan, 1970; Sattler, 1997). In particular, feminist educational scholarship establishes the importance of life histories when examining teachers and activism. Casey's (1993) study of women teacher activists used in-depth life history interviews to illuminate the various discourses invoked by the teachers when they talk about their lives and their work. For the teachers she studied, "everything is political" (Gramsci in Casey, 1993, p. 158). From the state and institutions as sites of political struggle to the negotiation of personal identity and relationships, the lives and work of teacher activists are complexly grounded in particular social relationships and contexts (Casey, 1993). Building upon Casey, Sattler (1997) studied the politics and practices of feminist teaching and stresses the important position that teachers hold in society as actors for social change. Her analysis of how feminist teachers talk about what they do, illuminates the practical manifestations of the personal within the political and professional work of teaching (Sattler, 1997).

Both of these studies are indebted to Weiler's (1988) work studying women high school teachers whose lives reveal the dialectical relationship between "subject and object, consciousness and reality, thought and being" (Freire in Weiler, 1988, p. 73). "In their lives," Weiler (1988) writes, "we can see the outline of the structural forces that have in some sense acted upon and created these women, but we also see their own growing and developing consciousness of the world they have inherited and their own choices and actions to change that world" (p. 73). The teachers in each of these feminist studies were all influenced by family histories, their own schooling experiences, wider social movements and other events, structural constraints, and forces of hegemony, all of which led them to take actions in their lives and in their teaching as subjective actors and agents of change.

Teacher Union Activism

Historically, the most recognized way for teachers to act collectively has been to organize through their unions. Early 20th-century teacher union leaders like Margaret Haley in Chicago and the struggles to assert female leadership and voice within the National Education Association (NEA)—which functioned more as a professional association as opposed to a labor union in its early days—further underscore the connections between feminist activism and teacher activism. In addition, applying the lenses of critical resistance and social justice education to historical teacher union activism emphasizes that teachers have long been in positions of political significance and engaged in activist efforts to effect social change.

For example, Levine (2002) discussed, in detail, the Milwaukee Teachers Association's 1920s opposition to what members saw as the "factoryizing" standardization of education. In an education policy context eerily similar to today's, Milwaukee teachers organized against corporate business influence on public school reform. The 2011 election of longtime social justice unionism advocate Bob Peterson as president of the Milwaukee Teachers Education Association (MTEA) underscores the tradition and commitment that Milwaukee teachers have displayed in working to align their interests with those of the families, students, and communities they serve (Peterson, 1999; 2011).

Teacher union organizing efforts in New York City in the 1930s and 1940s were also strongly tied to community activism and an alternative vision for education. Johnson (2002) chronicled the Teachers Union of New York City's activism during these two decades that focused largely on "progressive curriculum projects and grassroots involvement in school reform," noting that "schools were a primary site for social change" where progressive and radical educators and civil rights activists worked together to promote "Black history and intercultural curriculum materials, advocated hiring more African-American teachers and administrators, and worked side-by-side with parents for school reform in predominately Black neighborhoods such as Harlem and Bedford-Stuyvesant" (pp. 567–568). The New York City union activists displayed the same skills that Levine outlined for teacher activists in Milwaukee: research and policy analysis, forging alliances with community allies, and articulating an alternative educational vision.

The clear ties that early 20th-century urban teachers' unions were able to make between their interests and those of students and urban communities unraveled in the face of post-World War II antiunionism and exacerbated racial tensions spanning from the 1950s to the 1970s (Johnson, 2002; Levine, 2002; Perrillo, 2012; Urban, 1989). The New York City teacher strikes in 1968 stemming from controversy over establishing Black community control of schools in Harlem and Ocean Hill-Brownsville serve as a lasting symbol of the decay of trust and partnership between majority White teaching forces and urban communities of color (Gordon, 2001; Perrillo, 2012; Urban, 1989). Enduring impressions, that teachers and their unions do not care for the communities where they teach, are motivated by issues of job security more than justice and are willing to sacrifice the interests of students for their own selfish ones, contribute to the oversimplified framing of "bad teachers" as the ones to blame for failing schools (Kumashiro, 2012).

The Chicago Teachers' Union (CTU) and its 2012 strike provide an important example of teachers acting collectively to push back against larger systemic education reforms from a wider social justice perspective (Sokolower, 2012). Significantly, widespread public support across the city of Chicago for the CTU's decision to go on strike included the majority of public school parents and many grassroots community activist organizations (Chicago Teachers Union, 2012). In 2015, Seattle teachers went on strike over issues that included numerous student-centered demands related to testing, recess, student support services, and equitable learning opportunities (Bryant, 2015). Further, there is a renewed focus on the idea of social justice unionism among union activists (GEM NYC, n.d.; Rethinking Schools, 2012; Sokolower, 2012) and both the American Federation of Teachers (AFT) and NEA are seeking collaboration and alliances with parent and community activist and organizing groups (Catone, 2013; McAlister & Catone, 2013). These efforts represent the potential for teacher union activism to center broader social justice aims.

New Grassroots Teacher Activism

In a nonunion context, Marshall and Anderson (2009) conducted a study of 52 "activist educators" in North Carolina and uncovered a few particularly concerning challenges. First, they found that the most widely used strategy by educator activists to "continue their careers and, at the same time, retain identification with a social justice cause" (Marshall & Anderson, 2009, p. 141) was "keeping it on the down-low…devis[ing] clever strategies to enact activism quietly" (p. 143). Further, educator activists found little space for acting publicly in local contexts and often felt alone and isolated. The authors concluded that "absent opportunities for collaboration, networking, and mutual support of shared values, much power and sustenance is lost" (Marshall & Anderson, 2009, p. 160).

The narrative of isolated teacher activists is not unique. In an article published in the trade magazine, *Teaching Tolerance*, the author interviewed seven "activist teachers" who all expressed "that lonely feeling" as ones who stand up for equity and speak out against injustice (Teaching Tolerance, 1999). In part, feelings of isolation are what led a small group of teachers in New York City to come together to form the grassroots teacher activist group, New York Collective of Radical Educators (NYCoRE) (Catone, Mangual Figueroa, & Picower, 2010). Similar groups have formed across the country (Au, et. al., 2005; Doster, 2008) and many are connected to each other through the national network of Teacher Activist Groups (TAG). A limited amount of literature suggests that they provide effective platforms to connect teacher activists who might otherwise feel isolated and support collective teacher activism (Oakes & Rogers, 2006; Picower, 2007; Rogers, et al., 2009).

Montaño and colleagues (2002) found that teacher activists articulate a dialectic relationship between the work they do outside of their classrooms and their sense of purpose and responsibility to their students inside of their classrooms: "For these teachers, simply being a 'good' (that is, a social justice) teacher within the four walls of their own classrooms was not enough. ...Their sense of the strategic necessity of a social movement remained rooted in the needs of inner-city students and in particular the students in their own classrooms, who continue to give their struggle meaning and urgency" (Montaño, et al., 2002, p. 272). Similarly, Picower (2012) found that the most committed teacher activists were ones who were active both inside and outside their classrooms. They saw their roles as teacher activists to both teach their students in ways to support liberatory change and take part in activism, especially education activism, outside their classrooms to "practice what they teach" (Picower, 2012, p. 109). In fact, she also found that teachers with less-developed activist outlooks, who do impressive work to integrate social justice into their classroom teaching, often get "stuck at the classroom door," dangerously "falling back on tools of inaction" (Picower, 2012, p. 71).

Teacher activists recognize a simultaneous need to build empowered, democratic spaces in their classrooms and build collective power with others outside of schools. Numerous scholars have raised the argument that an organized educational justice movement is necessary to challenge social inequities, maintain the democratic promise of public education, and assert the freedom and liberation of low-income communities and communities of color in the United States (Anyon, 2005; Lipman, 2011; Oakes & Rogers, 2006; Perry, et al., 2010). Teacher activists are among those forming such a movement as many articulate their work as connected to a larger social movement for educational justice (Picower, 2012; 2013). The current literature helps us understand what might be the purpose of an educational justice movement and even gives us examples of what it might look like from teachers' perspectives. But it does not deeply examine the individual motivations for how and why teachers come to be engaged in such work. For an educational justice movement to grow and for it to include teachers, it will be important to understand how and why teachers become activists in the first place.

Framing Teacher Activists

Ultimately, the pedagogy presented in this book is derived from individual portraits of four teacher activists. The portraits explore their political development and journeys in becoming teachers and activists, the visions and purposes for their work, and the ways in which their activist outlooks, teaching philosophies, and educational justice objectives manifest in practice. As I constructed these portraits, two areas of scholarship provided valuable frames through which to view and understand each individual's stories: (1) social movement theories about how and why people become activists and (2) overlapping literature on critical pedagogy and social justice education.

Becoming an Activist

Social movements literature has widely explored questions of why and how people become activists. Theories that connect social movement activism to the self-interested promise of personal psychological gain (Hoffer, 1951) or to narrow conceptions of economic incentives and entrepreneurial gain (Moe, 1980) have been extensively applied, but have also been shown to gloss over more nuanced and complex factors motivating activists to become engaged in their work (Teske, 1997). While surely some sense of self-worth and meaning is derived from teacher activism and there is a level of interest group incentive that impacts the work, these are inadequate explanations for such deeply personal, professional, and political action. More compelling are theories focused on moral and developmental models that explain why and how people become engaged in activism.

The emotional violation of a person's sense of justice can be the impetus for becoming an activist. Jasper (1997) describes "moral shocks" as "an unexpected event or piece of information [that] raises such a sense of outrage in a person that she becomes inclined toward political action.... The information or event helps a person think about her basic values and how the world diverges from them in some important way" (p. 106). Similarly, Teske (1997) stressed at the impact of "moral discoveries" resulting from "some external shock to the self. ...The moral discoveries described by activists are often vision-altering gestalts and revelatory epiphanies, not mere factual observations. ...[T]hey combine some new insight into the nature of the world with a new paradigm for understanding how one ought to act and live one's life" (p. 55). Warren (2010) talks about how "seminal experiences" of White racial justice activists "are accompanied by powerful emotions, typically anger or outrage at injustice. These experiences make Whites aware, for the first time, of the reality of racism. They lead to righteous anger for the very reason that racist practice violates the values of justice and equality with which these people had been brought up and in which they deeply believe" (p. 27). These studies highlight how moments of moral dissonance between a person's core values or belief system and a personal encounter with injustice are often key factors for one's activist development.

Related to the idea of development, Warren (2010) noted that while there is a tendency to focus on single decision points at which activists join particular movements, the development of commitment is a process which grows over time rather than a one-time conversion. Teske's (1997) discussion of activists' tendency to tell "'involvement stories,' dramatic narrative accounts of the development of their political activism," (p. 34) supports the idea that becoming an activist happens over time, combining themes of personal crisis, moral discovery, and lifelong commitment. Activist commitment is the subject of Andrews's (1991) study of 15 longtime activists whose "becoming and being committed was, and is, a process" (p. 143) influenced by factors causing a transformation of the way in which one understands her lived experience over the course of her lifetime. Thus, it is just as important to understand the development of life histories as it is to uncover moments of moral shock or discovery when explaining why people become activists.

However, activists are supported by more than their own personal convictions, experiences, and inclinations. Andrews (1991) identifies three influences in activating political consciousness: identifiable individuals who act as models or inspiration, intellectual stimulants (such as books, movies, formal and informal education), and examples of activism supported by highly visible organizations. Additionally, McAdam and Paulsen's (1993) research on participation in the Civil Rights Movement stresses that attitudinal affinity or predispositions to engage, while important, are not enough to explain why people get involved in social movement activism. Interpersonal ties and organizational affiliations are crucial, and further, these elements only have predictive power in determining whether someone will engage in activism when they reinforce "a strong subjective identification with a particular identity" (McAdam & Paulsen, 1993, p. 659).

For example, teachers were specifically recruited to engage in the Freedom Summer project of 1964, a major effort in Black communities in the South to conduct citizenship education and voter registration through "freedom schools." Organizers specifically recruited teachers by gaining endorsements from both national teachers' unions and approaching education majors on college campuses (McAdam & Paulsen, 1993). These efforts linked teacher identities with participation in the movement. In other words, the structural circumstances of the Freedom Summer project and the identification of the need for teachers in particular had just as much to do with the involvement of teachers as any given teacher's predisposition or moral imperative to get involved. As we further examine the inner motivations and development of teacher activists, it is also important to identify, understand, and describe the external influences that also facilitate their activism.

Teaching to Change the World

Whether or not they become activists, a popular refrain for explaining why people want to become teachers is because they want to "make a difference" in the world. In terms of difference making, critical theorists have long posited that schools and education help reproduce dominant social orders, class structures, and privileged cultural and linguistic patterns (Anyon, 1980; Apple, 1982; Bernstein, 1975; Bourdieu & Passeron, 1977; Bowles & Gintis, 1977; Giroux, 2001; Heath, 1983; MacLeod, 1995; McLaren, 2007; Willis, 1981). Yet a lot of the earliest works that established social reproduction theory have been criticized for being overly deterministic, treating teachers and students as passive actors in systems so powerful that they inevitably reproduce hierarchical relations. The exploration of the tension and relationship between structure and agency builds the foundation for critical pedagogy and the essential roles that teachers play in upholding and/or challenging status quo power relations in society.

Weiler (1988) discusses the tension between structure and agency in critical analyses by teasing out what she calls "theories of production," by which she means theories that "are concerned with the ways in which both individuals and classes assert their own experience and contest or resist the ideological and material forces imposed upon them in a variety of settings" (p. 11). She encourages a focus on "the ways in which both teachers and students in school produce meaning and culture through their own resistance and their own individual and collective consciousness" (p. 11). In particular, Freire (1993) and Giroux (2001) offer theories of critical pedagogy that recognize the essential agency of teachers in efforts to change—rather than reproduce—society.

Freire (1993) understood and theorized "education as the practice of freedom" (p. 62). He poses an approach to education that "affirms men and women as beings in the process of *becoming*—as unfinished, uncompleted beings in and with a likewise unfinished reality" (p. 65). Becoming free for Freire is synonymous with becoming human and rests upon the development of a deepened critical consciousness such that people "apprehend [their] situation as an historical reality susceptible of transformation" (p. 66). A "humanizing pedagogy" (Bartolomé, 1994) treats teachers and students not as objects incapable of their own decision-making, but instead as subjects who can act as agents of change.

Giroux's work extensively discussed acts of resistance by school-based actors as challenges to dominant and oppressive structures. In a critique of reproduction theories, Giroux (2001) writes that the "existence of dominant ideologies and structural constraints in schools do not mean that educational outcomes are a passive reflex" and continues to point out that reproduction theories are limited in their "undialectical notion of power," the idea that "power works on people rather than through them" (p. 225). He points out that the dominant ideologies and power structures, that reproduction theorists find so pervasive, can be mediated by classroom practice, or pedagogy. Thus, Giroux (1992) theorizes resistance, in part, as teachers being "cultural workers" positioned in classrooms where they have the power and agency to mediate cultural production that might otherwise replicate dominant power relations.

In the struggle to reinvent rather than reproduce society, and in response to the charge that critical pedagogy makes of teachers to be "social and moral agents" (McLaren, 2007, p. 254), efforts to support social justice education are practical manifestations of teaching for change. The project of social justice education takes two major forms: analysis and action. First, "social justice includes a vision of society in which the distribution of resources is equitable and all members are physically and psychologically safe and secure" (Adams, Bell, & Griffin, 1997, p. 3). Central to this social justice vision is an educational approach that analyzes and critiques current inequitable distributions of resources. Inequities are most commonly exposed as outcomes of the systemic oppression of various groups through social "-isms" that maintain power imbalances (Adams, Bell, & Griffin, 1997). The exposure of these "-isms" can work to raise people's critical consciousness who will then be more likely to both imagine and work for a transformed, just society. Second, social justice education "serves as a reminder not only of the inequities and biases that continue to wear away at the foundation of democratic values, but the powerful stories which inspire us to work toward change, to make the world a better place" (Hunt, 1998, p. xiii). Social justice education focuses heavily on the ways in which teachers can facilitate learning to prepare students to become democratic citizens with critical consciousness aimed at taking action to create a more socially just world.

Further underscoring the action-orientation of social justice education Ayers (1998) stresses "teaching for social justice is teaching that arouses students, engages them in a quest to identify obstacles to their full humanity, to their freedom, and then to drive, to move against those obstacles" (p. xvii). This message is virtually the same as Payne's (2008) simple definition of education for liberation as "those forms of education intended to help people think more critically about the social forces that shape their lives and think more confidently about their ability to react against those forces" (pp. 1–2). Freire (1993) believed that freedom was the central focus of education in response to a society predicated upon practices of domination, establishing "the theme of *liberation* as the objective to be achieved" (p. 34). Finally, critical pedagogy and social justice education are as much about living and being as they are about teaching. In the examination of "lived examples of critical pedagogy," Duncan-Andrade and Morrell (2008) emphasize "that critical pedagogy is more than just a teaching strategy—it is a personal, financial, political, emotional, and spiritual commitment to prioritizing the needs and liberation of people who are suffering under various forms of oppression" (p. 37).

No matter the particular focus, one consistent reality is underscored by social justice and liberatory education and also reinforced by the foundational work of critical theorists: education is political and, therefore, teaching can never be neutral. Hoo (2004) calls upon teachers and teacher educators to "become 'subjects' of history and not 'objects' that simply watch the world go by" (p. 209). If there is one characteristic that teacher activists have in common, it is that they are, at the very least, all *doing* something, taking explicit action.

Creating Portraits

Sattler (1997) observed a "dialectic of structural constraint and personal autonomy" (p. 88) in her study of feminist teachers. My research questions were designed to capture important pieces of this dialectic: how teacher activists understand and explain the development of their teaching and activism, how they attempt to put their activist commitments into practice, the challenges they face in doing their work, and how they sustain and support these commitments.

I needed a methodology that was powerful enough to capably explore teachers' beliefs, motivations, everyday lives, life histories, classroom practice, community activism, and more. To meet these demands, I turned to portraiture.

Portraiture blends elements of art and science to search "for what is good and healthy" (Lawrence-Lightfoot & Davis, 1997, p. 9). A powerful rhetoric of "bad teachers, bad schools, and broken systems" has propelled recent standards-based, market-driven education reform efforts (Simmons, 2013). Kumashiro (2012) pointed out how the current "common sense" standards-based and market-driven framing of school reform has supported the notion that good teachers are those who can raise student test scores. As a result, he writes, "When we narrowly define the good teacher merely in terms of the ability to raise test scores, we inevitably are categorizing all others as bad, even those who, in so many other ways, are successful, admirable, valuable, impactful, effective, ethical, and good" (Kumashiro, 2012, p. 21). Portraiture's focus on an expansive search for goodness, as opposed to the diagnostic identification of pathology, takes on significant importance in an education reform context that so narrowly defines "good" teaching.

I use portraiture to expand and enlarge what might be considered good teaching by asking, "What is good here?" of teacher activists and assume "the expression of goodness will always be laced with imperfections" (Lawrence-Lightfoot & Davis, 1997, p. 9). The data I collected were rich. I conducted two in-depth, semistructured, one-on-one interviews with each participant during the 2008–2009 school year (Seidman, 2006). In addition, I conducted three more in-depth interviews with each participant during the 2010–2011 school year. While my initial interviews were semistructured to focus on personal life histories, the later interviews were loosely structured in order to ask questions based on my ongoing analysis, information gathered in previous interviews, and reflections upon the many observations made throughout the same school year. I visited teachers on a monthly basis throughout the 2010–2011 academic year, spending at least 40 hours with each in various settings, including their classrooms, teaching and/or activist meetings, political events outside of school, conferences, and social settings such as after-work happy hours or dinner gatherings after evening meetings. I also collected documents from each participant, such as lesson/unit plans and materials, meeting agendas, event fliers, and conference programs.

I anticipated that my data would be rife with subtlety and contradiction as I talked to and observed teacher activists who expressed desires to teach and act in ways that further educational and social justice, but then operated within the "dialectic of structural constraint and personal autonomy." Rather than see contradictions and inconsistencies as problems to overcome, portraiture embraces them as "the complexity, dynamics, and subtlety of human experience" (Lawrence-Lightfoot & Davis, 1997, p. xv). Additionally, unlike dominant research paradigms that go to great lengths to remove or minimize the presence of the researcher, portraiture actively recognizes that presence and incorporates it into the methodological elements of design, data collection, analysis, and writing. My own history and relationship with teacher activism in New York City, then, is not a source of detrimental bias, but a point of reference that can be used to advantage my researcher perspective and analysis. At the same time, I wrestle with my affinity and admiration for the teacher activists in my study and my responsibilities as a researcher to maintain a disciplined skepticism, requiring authentic empirical evidence for the findings and conclusions I present. Portraiture is designed to work with and manage the tension between personal predisposition and rigorous skepticism.

Its richness as a methodology serves as a metaphor for portraiture's utility in the exploration of complex phenomena. Given the breadth of teacher activism's complexity and the depth of understanding, necessary to uncover the level of detail required by my research questions, portraiture seemed an obvious choice. The overall portraiture process was incredibly humbling. The privilege that I have in being allowed to tell the stories of four great teacher activists is one that I only accept with immense recognition of my responsibility. It is my hope that readers will agree that I have adequately fulfilled this responsibility without undue exercise of my privileges as portraitist and that the participants resonate with and recognize themselves in what I have written. With that, I submit the following four portraits of Rosie Frascella, Natalia Ortiz, Kari Kokka, and Lisa North.

References

Adams, M., Bell, L.A., & Griffin. P. (eds.). (1997). *Teaching for diversity and social justice: A sourcebook.* New York: Routledge.

Andrews, M. (1991). *Lifetimes of commitment: Aging, politics, psychology.* Cambridge, UK: Cambridge University Press.

Anyon, J. (1980). Social class and the hidden curriculum of work. *Journal of Education, 162*(1), 67–92.

Anyon, J. (2005). *Radical possibilities: Public policy, urban education, and a new social movement.* New York: Routledge.

Apple, M. (1982). *Education and power.* London: Routledge & Kegan Paul.

Au, W., Bigelow, B., Burant, T., & Salas, K.D. (2005). Teacher organizers take quality into their own hands. *Rethinking Schools.* Retrieved May 13, 2007 from http://www.rethinking schools.org/archive/20_02/orga202.shtml

Ayers, W. (1998). Popular education: Teaching for social justice. In W. Ayers, J.A. Hunt & T. Quinn (eds.), *Teaching for social justice* (pp. xvii–xxv). New York: The New Press and Teachers College Press.

Bartolomé, L.I. (1994). Beyond the methods fetish: Toward a humanizing pedagogy. *Harvard Educational Review,* 64(2), 173–195.

Bernstein, B. (1975). *Class, codes, and control.* London: Routledge and Kegan Paul.

Bourdieu, P. & Passeron, J.C. (1977). *Reproduction in education, society and culture.* London: Sage Publications.

Bowles, S. & Gintis, H. (1977). *Schooling in capitalist America: Educational reform and the contradictions of economic life.* New York: Basic Books.

Bryant, J. (2015, September 18). Seattle teachers' strike a win for social justice. Retrieved June 16, 2016, from https://ourfuture.org/20150918/seattle-teachers-strike-a-win-for-social-justice

Casey, K. (1993). *I answer with my life: Life histories of women teachers working for social change.* New York: Routledge.

Catone, K. (2013). Teachers unions as partners, not as adversaries. *Voices in Urban Education,* 36, 52–58.

Catone, K.C., Mangual Figuera, A., & Picower, B. (2010, May). *The beautiful struggle: Teacher activism as professional development.* Paper presented at the Annual Meeting of the American Education Research Association, Denver, CO.

Chicago Teachers Union. (2012). As Chicago teachers strike enters fourth day, a new poll proves majority of parents and taxpayers approve of fair contract fight. Retrieved September 15, 2012, from http://www.ctunet.com/blog/new-poll-shows-that-that-majority-of-the-public-supports-the-strike

Collins, P.H. (2009). *Black feminist thought: Knowledge, consciousness, and the politics of empowerment.* New York: Routledge Classics.

Doster, A. (2008, February 25). The conscious classroom: A new generation of educators, frustrated with ineffective reforms, turns to pedagogy focused on social justice. *The Nation.* Retrieved October 22, 2012, from http://www.thenation.com/article/conscious-classroom

Duncan-Andrade, J.M.R. & Morrell, E. (2008). *The art of critical pedagogy: Possibilities for moving from theory to practice in urban schools.* New York: Peter Lang.

Freire, P. (1993). *Pedagogy of the oppressed.* New York: Continuum.

Giroux, H.A. (1992). *Border crossings: Cultural workers and the politics of education.* New York: Routledge.

Giroux, H.A. (2001). *Theory and resistance in education: Towards a pedagogy for the opposition.* Westport, CT: Bergin & Garvey.

Gordon, J.A. (2001). *Why they couldn't wait: A critique of the Black-Jewish conflict over community control in Ocean Hill-Brownsville (1967–1971).* New York: Routledge Falmer.

Grassroots Education Movement (GEM) NYC. (n.d.). About us. Retrieved October 22, 2012, from http://gemnyc.org/about

Heath, S.B. (1983). *Ways with words*. Cambridge, UK: Cambridge University Press.

Hoffer, E. (1951). *The true believer*. New York: Harper & Row.

Hoo, S.S. (2004). We change the world by doing nothing. *Teacher Education Quarterly, 39*(1), 199–211.

Hunt, J.A. (1998). Of stories, seeds and the promises of social justice. In W. Ayers, J.A. Hunt & T. Quinn (eds.), *Teaching for social justice* (pp. xiii–xv). New York: The New Press and Teachers College Press.

Jasper, J.M. (1997). *The art of moral protest: Culture, biography, and creativity in social movements*. Chicago: University of Chicago Press.

Johnson, L. (2002). "Making democracy real": Teacher union and community activism to promote diversity in the New York City public schools, 1935–1950. *Urban Education, 37*(5). 566–587.

Kumashiro, K.K. (2012). *Bad teacher: How blaming teachers distorts the bigger picture*. New York: Teachers College Press.

Lawrence-Lightfoot, S. & Davis, J.H. (1997). *The art and science of portraiture*. San Francisco: Jossey-Bass.

Levine, D. (2002). The Milwaukee platoon school battle: Lessons for activist teachers. *The Urban Review, 34*(1), 47–69.

Lipman, P. (2011). *The new political economy of urban education: Neoliberalism, race, and the right to the city*. New York: Routledge.

MacLeod, J. (1995). *Ain't no makin' it: Aspirations and attainment in a low-income neighborhood*. Boulder, CO: Westview Press.

Marshall, C. & Anderson, A.L. (eds.). (2009). *Activist educators: Breaking past limits*. New York: Routledge.

McAdam, D. & Paulsen, R. (1993). Specifying the relationship between social ties and activism. *American Journal of Sociology, 99*(3), 640–667.

McAlister, S. & Catone, K.C. (2013). Real parent power: Relational organizing for sustainable school reform. *National Civic Review, 102*(1), 26–32.

McLaren, P. (2007). *Life in schools: An introduction to critical pedagogy in the foundations of education* (5th ed.). Boston: Pearson Allyn and Bacon.

Moe, T. (1980). *The organization of interests: Incentives and the internal dynamics of political interest groups*. Chicago: University of Chicago Press.

Montaño, T., López-Torres, L., DeLissovoy, N., Pacheco, M., & Stillman, J. (2002). Teachers as activists: Teacher development and alternate sites of learning. *Equity & Excellence in Education, 35*(3), 265–275.

Morgan, R. (ed.). (1970). *Sisterhood is powerful: An anthology of writings from the women's liberation movement*. New York: Random House.

Oakes, J. & Rogers, J. (2006). *Learning power: Organizing for education and justice*. New York: Teachers College Press.

Payne, C.M. (2008). Introduction. In C.M. Payne & C.S. Strickland (eds.), *Teach freedom: Education for liberation in the African-American tradition* (pp. 1–11). New York: Teachers College Press.

Perrillo, J. (2012). *Uncivil rights: Teachers, unions, and race in the battle for school equity.* Chicago: The University of Chicago Press.

Perry, T., Moses, R.P., Wynne, J.T., Cortes Jr., E. & Delpit, L. (eds.). (2010). *Quality education as a constitutional right: Creating a grassroots movement to transform public schools.* Boston: Beacon Press.

Peterson, B. (1999). Survival and justice: Rethinking teacher union strategy. In B. Peterson & M. Charney (eds.), *Transforming teacher unions: Fighting for better schools and social justice* (pp. 11–19). Milwaukee, WI: Rethinking Schools.

Peterson, B. (2011, September 21). *It's time to re-imagine and reinvent the MTEA.* Speech presented at Milwaukee Teachers Education Association Convocation, Milwaukee, WI. Retrieved September 3, 2013, from www.mtea.org/Public/pdf/Re-imaginespeech.pdf

Picower, B. (2007). Supporting new educators to teach for social justice: The critical inquiry project model. *Penn Perspectives on Urban Education, 5*(1). Retrieved September 15, 2012, from http://www.urbanedjournal.org/node/147

Picower, B. (2012). *Practice what you teach: Social justice education in the classroom and the streets.* New York: Routledge.

Picower, B. (2013). Education should be free! Occupy the DOE!: Teacher activists involved in the Occupy Wall Street movement. *Critical Studies in Education, 54*(1), 44–56.

Rethinking Schools. (2012). New teachers' union movement in the making. *Rethinking Schools, 27*(2), 5–6.

Rogers, R., Mosley, M., Kramer, M.A., & the Literacy for Social Justice Teacher Research Group. (2009). *Designing socially just learning communities: Critical literacy education across the lifespan.* New York: Routledge.

Sattler, C.L. (1997). *Talking about a revolution: The politics and practice of feminist teaching.* Cresskill, NJ: Hampton Press, Inc.

Seidman, I. (2006). *Interviewing as qualitative research: A guide for researchers in education and the social sciences.* New York: Teachers College Press.

Simmons, W. (2013, April 9). *The Annenberg Institute at 20: Executive director Warren Simmons looks back at two decades of school reform.* Retrieved January 8, 2014, from http://annenberginstitute.org/commentary/2013/04/annenberg-institute-20-executive-director-warren-simmons-looks-back-two-decades-s

Sokolower, J. (2012). Lessons in social justice unionism: An interview with Chicago Teachers Union president Karen Lewis. *Rethinking Schools, 27*(2), 10–17.

Teaching Tolerance. (1999). A solitary struggle. *Teaching Tolerance, 16.* Retrieved September 15, 2012, from http://www.tolerance.org/magazine/number-16-fall-1999/solitary-struggle

Teske, N. (1997). *Political activists in America: The identity construction model of political participation.* Cambridge, UK: Cambridge University Press.

Urban, W.J. (1989). Teacher activism. In D. Warren (ed.), *American teachers* (pp. 190–209). New York: Macmillan.

Warren, M.R. (2010). *Fire in the heart: How white activists embrace racial justice.* New York: Oxford University Press.

Weiler, K. (1988). *Women teaching for change: Gender, class & power.* Westport, CT: Bergin & Garvey.

Willis, P. (1981). *Learning to labor: How working class kids get working class jobs.* New York: Columbia University Press.

ROSIE FRASCELLA: CREATING SPACE

Part I: Safe Space

Rosie Frascella pushes a small cart piled high with her laptop, projector, and other class materials and teaching necessities—lesson planner, student work, worksheets, and handouts—packed into a set of folders. Standing tall at just about five foot three and bent forward to be able to push the cart, Rosie cannot see much in front of her, but she navigates the crowded hallways with ease, weaving back and forth amid heavy student foot traffic, relying upon the good sense of students to move out of the way. Dressed casually in brown khaki pants and a plaid buttoned shirt, her comfortable-looking, rubber-soled shoes help quick hallway maneuvers.

It was the start of Rosie's second year teaching at the International High School at Prospect Heights (IHSPS)—located just off Eastern Parkway—a wide thoroughfare in the heart of Brooklyn with pedestrian walkways separated from the busy center strip of road meant for through traffic and quieter side roadways where cars park and local traffic is funneled. The school is in a shared building, a common arrangement in New York City (NYC) as a result of large comprehensive high schools being broken apart into separate small schools within a single building. A marker of its longstanding history in the neighborhood, the building boasts an ornate stone façade characteristic of many old public school buildings in NYC. Wide stairways lead to the main doors and open to a grand entryway with high vaulted ceilings supported by stone columns on top of marble floors that lack their original sheen, but maintain their majestic character underneath the layers of dirt and grime that betray their age.

Juxtaposed with the age of the school building, the student population at IHSPS represents the residents newest to Brooklyn. As part of the Internationals Network for Public Schools, a student enters ninth grade at IHSPS only if he/she has lived in the United States for not more than four years. In the hallways, between classes, students gather in different groups, talking to friends as they walk to their next class. The diversity of student backgrounds is apparent from their physical appearance, with all shades of skin tone and every texture of hair imaginable, but it is the cacophony of languages that cascade upon my ears—those of a monolingual English speaker—that most clearly identifies the diversity of this student body. As Rosie and I make our way down the hall, I hear Arabic, Chinese, Spanish, and languages from Africa that my inadequately trained ears cannot identify. Rosie and I chat in English, which is clearly not the dominant language in this setting, but is the one common language for the student body.

We arrive at Rosie's 12th-grade social studies class, held in a room that is normally home to an English class as evidenced by the literary references posted on the walls defining metaphors and similes, personification and hyperbole. I settle into a seat toward the back half of the room and Rosie scrambles to set up the laptop and projector. She greets students as they began to stream into the classroom and take their seats. "Take out your homework for the Do Now," Rosie calls out as she finishes her tech set-up. "Find a partner to review your homework answers with."

The laptop and projector are important to the day's lesson. Students will watch the last part of an episode from the *National Geographic Taboo* documentary film series on "Sexuality," having already viewed the first half of the film in a previous class. The three main characters—Pashka, Lola, and Dawn—are transgender men and the film documents each of their decisions to consider sex reassignment surgery. The last time I saw Rosie, she was planning this unit with her social studies grade team. They had decided to explore the broad theme of "nature vs. nurture" and a unit challenging notions that gender identity is merely something biological and showing that it can also be something socially constructed would fit.

Rosie previews the second half of the documentary, highlighting that they will be exploring why so many people go to Thailand for sex reassignment surgery. Before cueing up the film, she quickly quizzes students on some statistics they had learned previously. "How many people identify as homosexual?" she asks. Students scan their notes and a few blurt out the answer "one in ten." "How about transgender?" Rosie continues. "One in 12,000," students quickly reply, most having located their notes. Rosie starts the film, projecting it from her laptop onto a screen set up at the front of the room. Students take notes in anticipation of a "notetaking quiz"—a handout that has incomplete pieces of information which students must fill in based on the notes they have from watching the film—before the end of class. Rosie pauses the film when a doctor states that most patients seeking sex reassignment surgery knew that they were transgender early in childhood and could often recall specific moments when they knew. "Did you all hear that part?" she asks her students. She pauses it again to reemphasize the point that "U.S. law requires years of psychotherapy" before someone can go through sex reassignment surgery and that in Thailand "transsexuals face no such restrictions."

Rosie turns off the projector with enough time left in the period for an open class discussion. First, disappointed that they did not watch until the end of the documentary, students make Rosie promise that they will see the end of the video in their next class. Then, the questions begin flowing freely from students' lips. "Wait, so now they all are gonna have a, you know, a […]" one student starts to say, faltering, embarrassed, until Rosie finishes the question with the answer, "A penis? Yes, they will each have a penis." "Will it work?" another student asks. There are nervous laughs and an occasional snicker, but overall students are genuinely interested and continue to ask questions about transgender identity and sex reassignment surgery.

There is some skepticism among her students and discomfort with the topic of conversation. One male student, who seems exasperated by the conversation, declares, "I'm not sayin' that there's anything wrong with it, but it [transgender identity and sex reassignment] just seems a little crazy and weird." Rosie does not say anything and instead two female students respond by saying, "It's not crazy" and "It's who they are." Students are also tripped up over which gender pronouns to use. One of the girls refers to Dawn as "she, uh, I mean, he, uh, I don't know!" Again, it is not Rosie who clarifies, but another student who calmly points out, "Well, it's he now, he is a man." In the end, the discussion is not about whether these things are morally right or wrong, as one might expect given the ways these topics enter into popular discourse. Instead, it is more about how the surgery works, how individuals live their lives afterward, and the functionality of the sex organs. For students in this discussion, the notion of someone identifying as transgender and potentially wanting sex reassignment surgery is closer to being accepted as a matter of fact, normal, and human.

Two years earlier, I sat with Rosie in a bustling coffee shop in Washington Heights, near Columbia University's Presbyterian Hospital. At the time, she was a second-year English as a Second Language (ESL) and English teacher at a high school in the neighborhood. When Rosie arrived, we launched into conversation without much pause or pretense. Just three minutes in, Rosie said, "I think that one of the things that really comes out to me in terms of my childhood is that at a really young age I knew I was gay." And it is to this early childhood experience that she attaches her first moment of politicization. "I think that's been a big part of how I was able to really deconstruct the world and realize that it's not the way everyone tells it to you," she continued. "So, in kindergarten and first grade I was openly gay, but I didn't know that I was gay; I just liked girls. I would tell people and girls liked me and it was like, whatever." But then by second grade, Rosie remembered something shifting and "knowing that I shouldn't talk about it, knowing that it was wrong." She stopped telling people that she liked girls and "just went in the closet and said that I would never be this. I would never be gay, I would just have to learn to love a man, or else I wouldn't love." She would not come out again until she was 17. Reflecting as an adult, Rosie sees this early moment of contradiction between what she knew about herself and what others taught her about the world as having planted the seeds of her disposition to deconstruct the world, exposing the lies in how reality and normality are presented.

Perhaps not coincidentally, second grade proved to be a trying time for Rosie. By her own account, she "got in a lot of trouble." "I would talk or something and [the teacher] would put my desk up against the wall," Rosie recalls. "There were times where I was literally in a cubicle, I couldn't see, they trapped me." In second grade, Rosie felt confined and targeted by teachers. One time, when out at recess, she was accused of making one of her classmates fall down in the mud. "I wasn't even near her!" Rosie pleaded with her teacher. "I didn't touch her or anything, and I got in trouble for it. It didn't matter that I said I didn't do it."

To Rosie, these negative school experiences are connected to a number of factors in her childhood. Rosie's mother left her father when Rosie was a baby. Her father "had a reputation" for being in trouble with the law and that reputation preceded Rosie and her older brothers when they arrived to school. In addition, there were not many children from single-parent households in her second-grade class. She was also stigmatized in other ways as a student who was pulled out of class to work with a speech therapist and carried a special education student label. Whether her teachers actually treated Rosie differently because of these things, her impression as an elementary school student was that they were mean to her and she tuned out from school. For example, when it was time to fill in bubbles on test answer sheets, Rosie pretended that A was racing B and C, randomly coloring in her test responses: "I was just doo-doo-doo, in my own imaginary world. I would play in my desk and have erasers be people. I was never paying attention. I was just not into school."

At the end of the year, Rosie and her mother were informed that Rosie would need to repeat second grade because she had gotten Fs in English and reading. But seeing her daughter suffer through second grade the first time, Rosie's mom fought against the school's decision. Naturally protective, Rosie's mom was not fond of the second-grade teacher's treatment of her daughter. A compromise was reached. Rosie's aunt, who was much younger than her mother and in college, would tutor her in English and reading over the summer. Then, Rosie could be promoted to third grade. It was a small victory; a proud moment for Rosie as she witnessed her mother sticking up for her against a teacher who was so mean. At this vulnerable point in Rosie's childhood, the way adults treated her seemed clear: her mother and aunt cared for her; her teachers did not.

Rosie did have teachers who seemed to relate to her with greater care. Starting with third grade, Rosie had one teacher who made her "feel really good" about herself and another, in fifth grade, who would "say really good things" and "was really positive." These teachers were "strict, but affirming" and Rosie felt like she "could participate" and "was part of a community." Whereas her other teachers made her feel "ostracized and separated from the rest of the class," these teachers made Rosie "feel safe." This safety helped Rosie trust her teachers, want to learn from them, and made her "not feel stupid." This contrasting treatment from teachers shaped much of Rosie's elementary school experience. As a student, she would not learn from teachers who did not take the time to see good things in her and make her feel safe. Thus, her early educational experiences led to a salient feature for Rosie in her teacher activist life: the creation of safe space.

The more popular idea of safe space comes out of the Lesbian, Gay, Bisexual, Transgender, Queer (LGBTQ) rights movement and, in general, is an idea upheld by activists working in solidarity with historically marginalized groups. In short, the dominant, mainstream space is often unsafe for individuals and groups that do not conform to that which is normalized and safe space challenges these norms. I recently had the opportunity to talk to a group of queer youth activists and asked them to reflect upon what kind of world their work is trying to bring into being. Their responses centered on the creation of a world where people are empowered to be who they want to be. They did not talk about this in a careerist sense, not that a person should be able to grow up and become a doctor or lawyer, but instead that people should live in a world that supports them to exist as they are. The ideas shared by these youths constitute the essence of the safe space that Rosie seeks.

As a child, being who she was already seemed out of the question as Rosie learned to hide her attraction to girls. The tragic suicide of a gay college student who faced harassment from his roommate at Rutgers University occurred just days prior to one of our meetings and triggered Rosie to talk about how a major problem for queer youth is that "these kids have no vision of what it is like to be an adult. I didn't have a vision for that growing up, either. I didn't know. How do you live as an older gay person, queer person?" The broader context of Rosie's working and middle-class hometown of Hamilton, New Jersey, was not the "type of town where you could express yourself and you could be different."

During her junior year in high school, one of Rosie's best friends had another good friend and Rosie "could see that they had this kind of relationship." She knew that they were both also gay and struggling with gender identity. One day, Rosie received a phone call from her friend, who told her that the other girl had hanged herself. She would find out later from her friend that the girl's suicide was related to a "*Romeo and Juliet* love tragedy." The girl had told Rosie's friend that she was gay and attracted to her, but Rosie's friend "couldn't deal with it and didn't say anything." "She was in shock and didn't know what to say," Rosie recalled. "She didn't say anything, she was quiet." The same day, the girl "came out to her parents and her parents couldn't deal with it." Rosie explained that her father was very religious and then shook her head as she told me that the girl hanged herself the next day. At school, "nobody talked about it, nobody said anything about being gay. Teachers didn't even talk about the suicide; there was just an empty desk. Everyone just kind of ignored it."

This memory stays with Rosie. In Hamilton, "there were no safe spaces. There was no space to say that you were gay." Whenever she hears about a young person committing suicide, she wonders if it is related to struggles with a queer identity. "I knew why she killed herself," Rosie reflected. "Because as a kid I, kind of, knew what she was struggling with. Keeping this secret where you know that you're never going to find love, or you think you're never going to be able to love anyone because it's not right. It puts a lot of pressure on you and it's easy to be like, well, why am I going to live?" For this reason, it is important to Rosie to be "out" as a teacher, to say to her students, "Look, I'm queer, I have a normal life, I have a job, I'm happy." Just as the youth activists I spoke with envision a future that includes them, Rosie assumes the responsibility to help her students understand that there is a future for each of them in a world that may not limit them in the ways that their current one seems to do. Rosie seeks to fulfill this responsibility as she creates a safe space in her work as a classroom teacher and teacher activist.

Part II: Activist Space

Rosie strives for her classroom to not just be a safe space, but also an activist space. "We talk about real issues. We talk about things in the world and we try to look critically at them," Rosie explains. "Critical thinking is a very valuable trait, a skill that we're supposed to teach our students. I try to use that. And then also just trying to get them active in their own community, not telling them what to think, but drawing out what are the issues, and helping them realize that you can create change. Trying to create activists in your students is being an activist." She recalls one unit from her second year of teaching that went particularly well in helping students think about their potential to be activists.

"We're never gonna eat at Burger King again," one small group of students exclaimed. "Yeah, I'm gonna tell my mom not to eat there, either," another student agreed. The students in Rosie's class were buzzing following a presentation by Alex Hernandez, a labor organizer working with tomato farm workers in Florida. Alex had just told them about a national campaign engaging farm workers, college students, and general consumers to fight for higher wages for workers who pick the tomatoes that find their way onto the sandwiches served by many U.S. fast food chains. Most recently, the campaign had successfully pressured Taco Bell to agree to pay an extra penny per pound of tomatoes, which would result in significant wage increases. The newest target was Burger King, which had not yet agreed to pay the extra penny per pound.

The class assignment for students was to write letters to Burger King expressing their views of the situation, connecting them to the novel the class had just finished reading, John Steinbeck's classic *The Grapes of Wrath*. "Miss, are we supposed to write our names at the end of the letter?" "Yeah, I don't want to leave my name or address—what if they come after us?" "You can leave mine if you don't want to put yours," Rosie smiled. "If anyone comes after us, then that means we're pretty bad ass, but I think we'll be safe." The students finished their letters, and some circulated a petition that Alex had left for them. Rosie collected all the paperwork and delivered it to Alex so that he could bring it down to Miami.

Three weeks later, news stories reported that Burger King caved from the pressure of the organized farm workers and their allies. The fast food chain joined its peers and agreed to pay the extra penny per pound of tomatoes. Rosie pulled up the farm worker's campaign website on a classroom computer to share the news of victory with her students. "We did that?!" some students exclaimed. "We were part of it," Rosie responded. The class erupted in cheers. By her account, this was one of the best units Rosie had ever taught. The students were invested in their learning and they got to "really understand what it's like to run a campaign, and their own power."

More than ten years earlier, Rosie was in high school and did not have any school experiences that helped her understand her own power. Instead, in 1997, when she was first accepted to college, Rosie still had not come out as gay and saw it as a chance for a fresh start, escaping the trauma of a community that had marginalized her for so long. She would be attending La Salle University, a Catholic institution in Philadelphia. Her first inclination was to "go there and remake myself," to be "more effeminate," and "find a boyfriend." But this is not what happened. Rosie came out before going to La Salle. She still keeps the notebook where she wrote for the first time that she was gay. "I actually wrote it down," she recalls. "I was 16 and a half, maybe 17 when I did that. And I came out maybe six months after that." Ironically, Rosie's time at La Salle did provide her the opportunity to remake herself, though not in the ways she had initially imagined. "La Salle was like my coming, my breaking through, you know," Rosie reflects. "It was the first time I was really known as a very positive contributor to my community."

Thrust into a Catholic institution that was unfriendly to queer identities because of religious doctrine, it seemed that being "out" would be a struggle at La Salle. Yet, much to her surprise, Rosie "met lots of gay people" at La Salle. During her sophomore year, Rosie and some other students started standing up to the university's exclusion of queer identities by "meeting and planning and thinking about starting a Gay-Straight Alliance and advocacy group."

University administrators told the students that they could have a group, but could not be affiliated with La Salle. Rosie and her peers decided to "step up our campaign." They went to the city paper, which agreed to write an article about the students' efforts to start a Gay-Straight Alliance (GSA) as a recognized student organization. The publicity forced La Salle to reconsider allowing the GSA to be affiliated with the school, and the group was established as an official student organization.

The GSA focused on planning activities and events asserting queer identity and helping LGBTQ members of the La Salle community carve out a safe space to explore questions about their sexual orientation, gender identities, and the Catholic faith. The events were closely monitored and scrutinized by the university's administration. "Everything we did had to get checked," Rosie recalls bitterly. "And I started to really see the hypocrisy in everything, especially in the administration." When the GSA planned an "antihate week" to raise awareness about discrimination and "all the -isms and oppression," university administrators requested to review agendas and plans for every event. The group organized a "Freedom to Marry Day," which consisted of holding short "commitment" ceremonies for people who could come and declare their commitment to anyone or anything. "They could commit to their teacher, they could commit to their pet, they could commit to their best friend, they could make any kind of commitment they wanted," Rosie explains. After people participated in these commitment ceremonies, GSA students handed them candy bars that included information about the right to marry in the United States on the wrappers. The message was aimed at helping people understand how marriage was treated as a privilege, only accessible to those privileged by their heterosexual relationships, and not as a right afforded to same-sex couples. La Salle University's name was included on the candy bar wrappers and university administrators "freaked out, they were like, 'This is not our position.' And after that, they were on us."

However, when fraternities and sororities were allowed to hold events like "Bid for Bodies" where dates with fraternity and sorority members were auctioned off to raise money, they were barely scrutinized at all. Falling securely within the dominant heterosexist norm, the university did not police these activities, even if students found them offensive and objectifying. The hypocrisy, Rosie identified in the administration's selective oversight of student groups, was an extension of what she sensed as a young child who knew that the way adults were presenting the world was not her reality. These moments, when adults in positions of authority conveyed to Rosie a depiction of the world she knew to be false, while in many ways paralyzing as a child, were radicalizing for her in college and served as the impetus for her launch into activism. They helped her develop an understanding that safe space is often achieved through struggle and the empowering potential of activism.

In addition, at La Salle, Rosie made an academic honor roll for the first time in her life. Her academic experience in college proved to be a far cry from high school when she "always got in trouble" and "would get kicked out of class" with a reputation as a "bad student." As opposed to some of her earlier school-ing experiences where she felt disliked by her teachers, Rosie says, "I got a lot of respect at La Salle. I still have teachers who call me. I was really respected for my work and my grades." La Salle became the space where her "confidence really started to build up" and Rosie realized that she "was capable and could succeed," which, according to her, was the first step in becoming an activist.

Rosie's academic work also opened up new horizons for her politically. Not having come from a family that was politically radical, Rosie felt that she was "definitely the black sheep of the family" and college was one of the first times she was exposed to more radical political thought. She took American history and literature classes and was assigned to read Allen Ginsburg's *Howl* and Tony Kushner's *Angels in America*, both texts that levy severe critiques on the dominant tropes of American history and society. As she pursued a mass-media public relations major, she read a lot of different things that opened her eyes "to the way media influence societal attitudes and the corruption in U.S. history." These ideas and perspectives were new to Rosie and so influential that, at 20 years old, she arrived for her senior year at La Salle in the fall of 2000 convinced that she needed to "get away." She realized that she "didn't know what was really out there" and "didn't have a really strong critique of global policy or the world or anything." Instead, she "knew that it was just luck or privilege that I was born in the United States and that I was White."

One way "to go experience life somewhere else" was to consider serving in the Peace Corps. Rosie applied and was selected. She was assigned to work in a remote village of 2,500 people in northern Mongolia. Her time abroad gave her a new perspective and Rosie "really started to understand the United States." She thought about "how privileged I was to even fight for gay rights, when these people are fighting just to survive [...]. Everyone had an extreme situation, of death, of abuse. And I started to see my privilege even more." Her time in the Peace Corps marked a real growth in Rosie's political consciousness, which would expand her sense of what it would mean to be an activist in the future as she became more sensitive to issues of power and privilege in the United States.

Without any immediate plans for work, Rosie went back to New Jersey after returning from Mongolia. While trying to determine what her next steps would be professionally, she took a seasonal, Christmas-time job at a local Barnes & Noble bookstore. She was not expecting this job to contribute to her growing political consciousness, but working near the bottom rungs of a huge corporate business set the stage for her next steps as an activist. One day, leading up to the Christmas holiday, the manager asked Rosie and her coworkers to "chip in and give money to the janitors who clean the building" for their Christmas bonus. "You asshole, why don't you just give them a bonus?" Rosie thought. "How much money did Barnes & Noble just make? And you're asking me, who makes eight dollars an hour, to give to janitors, who probably make seven dollars an hour?" Remembering her heated reaction, she says, "You know, it just really pissed me off and I got [a job] interview with the SEIU, Service Employees International Union."

Rosie was hired as an SEIU organizer and after some initial training and organizing work in New Jersey, she was sent to work on local campaigns in Los Angeles. From there she was moved to the San Francisco Bay Area in California. Following the model set by their lead organizer, her SEIU team in the Bay Area also became a team of local activists. The lead organizer would turn out to be one of Rosie's "first role models," offering Rosie a vision of an activist as "someone [who] does more than just go into work." Even though his job was a union organizer, "which by definition probably would be an activist," Rosie explains, "outside of his work he did what he was most passionate about and it didn't involve being paid for it." According to Rosie, he was "really radical; a White dude, but an amazing leader; one of the best organizers I've ever worked with." He was well connected in the Bay Area and very involved with a group of antiracist activists who organized workshops about facing White privilege and challenging White supremacy. His "strong political education background" guided Rosie's team through their own political education by reading different texts together. They developed self-critiques of the labor movement and looked for links to community organizing in the Bay Area. One of her other coworkers was a Filipina revolutionary who linked labor rights to support for a local Filipino community organization. These augmentations of their work meant that Rosie was putting in 12-hour days, working both to organize workers and to build solidarity and power with community groups. These experiences grounded her; everything she engaged with was "political" and it really made Rosie "feel more like an activist."

Rosie's work focused on organizing public sector employees, hospital workers, and childcare providers. "I kind of just got over my fear of talking to people," Rosie says. "Being a union organizer, you have to go out and knock on doors; you go out late at night by yourself, you go everywhere. I've been in Trenton, I've been in Compton, in Watts, all over the Bay Area. So, I've just seen so many different communities, all over." A far cry from Hamilton, New Jersey, the areas in which Rosie was spending time in organizing workers and building solidarity with people were low-income urban neighborhoods of color. She spent her long days in "working with workers and having them do collective actions and talking to their coworkers about their issues and being part of an [organizing] committee."

Rosie came to understand that talking with others about their experiences, worries, passions, and anger, and connecting people with similar stories, is a recipe for the creation of power. "First," Rosie says, "you always find the workers' issue. What are they passionate about?" Then, using that issue as a source of motivation, organizers "push" people "by testing their ability or their follow-through by giving them attainable tasks, a task that they can achieve." From there, organizers identify leaders to "use to either set the pace or to motivate [others]." Rosie came to see that "most people feel like they don't have any kind of power," but organizing "really affected their lives, really empowered them going through that process, especially if they won a contract and they saw the fruit of their labor." When she talks about the process of labor organizing, Rosie could just as easily be describing her classroom pedagogy.

After two years with SEIU, Rosie felt burnt out. She moved back to the East Coast and started doing some contract organizing, where she would get short-term assignments to go into different areas—largely in the chicken and meatpacking industry in Pennsylvania—to assess the viability for organizing unions at different work plants. But she did this work for only about a year, when she decided that she "wanted to go into social justice and education."

As much as Rosie "loved working with workers," she began to question herself, asking, "as a White woman from a middle-class background, what is my place in the movement? And who should I really be working with?" She reconsidered her role in social justice movement work and arrived at the following conclusion: "White women, that's who identify with me. That's who I am, that's my community." Rosie realized that White females make up the majority of the teaching force in the United States and this demographic reality first drew her to teaching. She thought she could work to help organize teachers to be a part of social justice movements. She found out about the Peace Corps Fellows program at Teachers College in NYC, which recruits returned Peace Corps volunteers into the teaching profession through an alternative certification program. Rosie applied, got in, and moved to NYC.

Reflecting on her path to becoming a teacher, Rosie tells me, "I came to teaching through wanting to be an activist. I wanted to be an activist first and a teacher second." Subsequently, Rosie sees her class as a space for students to not only feel safe and supported in looking critically at the world but also to dare to realize that they can actually change it. She also views teachers as potential activists for change in social justice movements, but recognizes that without being organized they may feel similar to the workers with whom she organized with SEIU—as if they do not have any power. Thus, Rosie's work as a teacher activist concentrates on creating empowering spaces for both teachers and students.

Part III: Empowering Teachers

Her colleagues jokingly refer to Rosie as "Rosie the Radical," a play on words in reference to "Rosie the Riveter," an iconic U.S. image from World War II of a woman in factory coveralls and her hair wrapped in a bandanna, calling out "We can do it!" with a pumped fist and flexed bicep meant to inspire women to take up factory work while men were away at war. "When I see a need or something that I think needs to be improved or something that I'm passionate about, I try to unite with other people to make it happen," Rosie says. "To try to create a mutual understanding and sharing tools and resources with people so we can empower each other." For someone who felt so disempowered for much of her youth, Rosie seems to be making up for lost time.

"Before I even started or moved to New York, I started looking up organizations," Rosie recalls. "I think people want to be part of a group. I think it's in our nature to want to belong to something [...] you can also get more people to do more work, if they feel invested in a group." She makes clear that as important as it is for her classroom to be a safe, activist, and empowering space promoting justice with her students, it is crucial that she not be a lone crusader and that she is "doing it with other people." In 2007, toward the start of her first year teaching, Rosie heard about New York Collective of Radical Educators (NYCoRE) when one of its leaders spoke at a Peace Corps Teaching Fellows graduate school class. She immediately got involved and now reflects,

"NYCoRE is really empowering for me, to be around other teachers that feel the same way I do, and where I can also gain resources and find out about different ways I can take things back to my classroom and just get support."

While interests broader than queer activism sparked her involvement, when she first started working with NYCoRE, Rosie's past activism around LGBTQ issues in college made her a ready leader for one of the organization's working groups, NYQueer. According to its website, NYQueer "focuses on gender and sexuality as they relate to school communities." The group works to "help teachers and schools in their efforts to form safe, inclusive environments that welcome and support individual differences of identity and self-expression." NYQueer meets regularly, organizes special events, creates curricular resource guides to support educators addressing LGBTQ issues, and organizes an annual gathering called Beyond Tolerance. Overall, Rosie believes that it is important to provide "support for teachers" and continue "creating conversations where we can share information to combat homophobia and transphobia in schools." As she knows from experience, this kind of work is not easy, especially when doing it within institutions that may not be supportive.

I attend NYQueer's first meeting of the 2010–2011 school year at the City University of New York (CUNY) Graduate Center in midtown Manhattan. The room itself is fairly nondescript, supplied with black rectangular tables and plastic chairs. The long fluorescent lights hanging from the ceiling remind me that I am in an institutional space, if the dingy industrial carpeting was not enough of a clue. Thirteen people are present, eight of them are new to NYQueer. Four attendees work at different community-based youth organizations and the rest are elementary and high school teachers, a high school guidance counselor, a college professor, and an unemployed teacher. Rosie opens the meeting with a brief overview of the group's history and then they go around to make introductions, asking people to share what it is that has brought them out to NYQueer. There seem to be three resonant themes voiced in their introductions. First, teachers are concerned with improving supports for queer youth in their schools. At least three of the teachers there are GSA advisors in their schools, and they are seeking to connect with other GSA leaders so that they can learn from each other. Second, the teachers themselves are seeking a community of support as queer teachers. One teacher believes that she was fired because she is a lesbian and was vocal about queer issues at her school. Others would like to be able to come to NYQueer as a space within which to feel empowered and share positive experiences and collectively strategize about how to break down barriers blocking LGBTQ activism in schools. Finally, there is widespread interest in connecting teachers and students with resources available through community-based organizations.

The interests and motivations for the educators attending the NYQueer meeting underscore the importance of safe, activist, and empowering spaces for teachers as well as students. To engage in the difficult work of building school environments supportive of queer students and staff, teachers need their own spaces from which to draw energy, support, and ideas. Each articulated interest, at the start of the meeting, emphasizes the need to connect with others who are engaged in similar struggles and the desire to feel more empowered in their work. As an organizer, Rosie had experience using unions to connect and empower workers and these experiences directly translated to why she decided to teach. "One of the main reasons I got into education was to do organizing work," Rosie reminds me. "I feel like there are a lot of issues in the world that need to be addressed that are gonna affect our kids, and we need to be united around these. And the only way that anything is gonna change is if we're involved in this process and educating other people around it." For teachers to gain a sense of the kind of power they could have, Rosie believes that they should not just come together through groups like NYQueer or NYCoRE but also through their union. In fact, she has posed the rhetorical question to me on more than one occasion, "If our union was better, would we need NYCoRE?"

Representing more than 200,000 members, the United Federation of Teachers (UFT) is the largest local affiliate of the national American Federation of Teachers (AFT). Its mammoth size makes it a powerful player in school reform debates in NYC. The potential teacher power, which Rosie envisions through the union, is "huge" and goes beyond its large membership. "Teachers' unions have some of the most power in the world among any other union because we have connections to the students and to the parents," Rosie explains. She believes that organizing teacher power is not all that teachers' unions should do—they should also "reach out to parents" and "get parents involved" because the school should be "the hub of a community." According to Rosie, "one of the big problems" for the UFT is that "in workplaces there are no issues" around which it is actively organizing. Her assessment is that the "UFT is not organizing anyone and they're operating on a service model [for example, exchanging dues payments for work benefits] and so that's what people think the union is for."

In February 2011, I receive an email from Rosie. It has a link to an archived radio show from two weeks earlier that aired a radio journalism piece she produced. Earlier in the school year, she took a radio journalism class to gain skills in media production. With her training from the class, Rosie produced a piece about school closings; the corporate, top-down management and reform style dominating NYC public schools; and the important role she sees for teachers' unions to organize and fight back. The piece aired on a local radio station, on the heels of community activism against school closings and the controversial appointment of Cathie Black as the NYC chancellor.

In November 2010, Chancellor of the NYC Department of Education (DOE) Joel Klein announced that he would be stepping down from his post in the midst of his ninth year on the job. Mayor Michael Bloomberg appointed Black, an education and public administration neophyte, to serve as the new schools chancellor starting in January. Activist groups swung into action looking to galvanize teacher and other education activists to push back against what they experienced as the top-down reforms of the Bloomberg education agenda.

Using her voice as the reporter-narrator, Rosie's radio segment offers a scathing critique of the NYC DOE policy of closing schools, especially those schools with deep historical roots in communities. Her measured journalistic voice still conveys her support for teacher activism. She compares New York's school closing policies to a similar reform approach in Chicago and discusses how such policies motivated teachers to form the Caucus of Rank-and-File Educators (CORE) to put "voice and democracy" back into the teachers' union. CORE was instrumental in raising the support to elect Karen Lewis as president of the Chicago Teachers Union in June 2010. Rosie highlights the work of Teachers Unite (TU), which brought CORE members from Chicago to speak at an event in NYC. She interviews a NYCoRE colleague who talks about the importance of teachers' unions connecting and organizing with the community and expresses the need for teachers to "take over the teacher unions and make them social justice unions." Rosie ends with a point I have heard from her before. "In New York, teachers are ready to be organized. And if the United Federation of Teachers doesn't do it, then educators will do it for themselves."

The points Rosie raises about the potential power of teachers through their union subscribe to a vision of social justice unionism, an idea promoted by progressive and radical teacher union activists since the 1990s. As articulated by Peterson and Charney (1999), social justice unionism envisions "a commitment to equity and excellence in education for all children" (p. 5). This vision includes "defending public education and the rights of teachers," "strong emphasis on professionalism," "commitment to children and community," "the question of union democracy and increased rank-and-file participation," and "bridging the divide" between "those who commit themselves to union activities and those who commit themselves to improving teaching practices by starting innovative schools, leading district curriculum committees, being active in the community, or participating in state and national professional organizations" (Peterson & Charney, 1999, p. 5). Ultimately, social justice unionism understands the union as a space from which teachers can work for change.

At the 2011 NYCoRE annual conference, I get the opportunity to learn more about Rosie's work with TU, a nonprofit organization devoted to organizing teachers to push for social justice unionism. TU director Sally Lee, a former core leader for NYCoRE, is facilitating a workshop called "The Only Way to Fight Back." One of the central questions the workshop explores is "What work should the UFT be doing to make it a social justice union?" Talking to other workshop participants, Rosie talks about building power with teachers. "There are pockets of teacher activism across the city, but teachers need to be organized as a whole. The UFT is really the only organization with the power and infrastructure to organize teachers at such a large scale," Rosie says. "The union needs to be TU, be NYCoRE; this conference should be organized by the union." Participants nod their heads in agreement.

Her comments spark discussion about how people consider what it means to "be the union" versus being subject to "the union leadership" and its decisions on their behalf. Participants want the union to both support their needs as teachers and fight for social justice. As a preliminary step, Rosie shares about how she has started teacher study groups at her school. She has gotten a team of teachers to dedicate some lunch breaks to discussing readings related to various educational issues in the city. Rosie described this strategy to me before in our interview back in the fall:

> I want to find a way to get my colleagues to think about these issues and have a discussion and to start thinking of our union differently. It's hard to understand the power of the union is not just about winning things or protecting yourself from your boss [...] [but] really seeing the power that our union could have to make systemic changes within New York, not just in education but at the roots, looking at the achievement gap and looking at where it stems from, poverty and housing and healthcare and jobs and all the other aspects that make our job a lot more difficult.

At the TU workshop, she is quite animated in her discussion of the possibilities of this approach, but also tempers expectations with the reflection that it
has been hard to move beyond the study group phase. In the end, Rosie and
her teacher activist colleagues understand that working to transform the UFT
is going to be a long, hard process, but they are fueled by the hopeful vision
of the powerful space, which a social justice union would be able to create for
teachers, schools, and communities to fight for change.

Just over two months after the NYCoRE conference, Rosie and I meet
to reflect on the school year. For much of our conversation, Rosie talks about
how overloaded she feels at work and by her activism. From the appointment
of Cathie Black to the recent slate of proposed school closings, it has been a
long school year for education activists. Remembering her tempered excitement at the NYCoRE conference about starting to organize teachers at her
school, I ask her how that is going. She tells me that it has been challenging.
"The thing is, everybody either is overworked, has a kid, or is checked out,
you know what I mean? So organizing them is just, I don't know [...]" Rosie
trails off with exasperation. "I don't have a core at my school. I'm isolated [...]
so I put in all this energy in and write these emails and try to get my staff to
do things and they don't show up and I don't have the energy during the day
to be running around." This is really the first time I have sensed any level of
defeat in Rosie and her frustration catches me somewhat off guard.[1]

One challenge for Rosie is balancing her involvement with different
teacher activist groups. She does not necessarily have the energy to work on
organizing teachers in her school because she is so engaged in different citywide efforts to bring teachers together. One promising part of the conversation is an update on some recent coalition work that involves a handful of the
grassroots teacher activist groups in NYC. Representing NYCoRE, Rosie has
attended a series of meetings that include members from TU, the Grassroots
Education Movement (GEM), and some other organizations. In its beginning
stages, the group has jokingly taken to calling itself "Voltron"—a reference
to a popular 1980s television cartoon about a team of space explorers whose
ships could come together and form a giant robot, Voltron, in order to defend
the universe from evil. Rosie says that at first she "wasn't very excited" about
Voltron, but after attending meetings she thinks that it has the potential to
be a "powerhouse." The coalition group is still determining its focus but has
started to hone in on working together to push the UFT closer toward being
a social justice union through forming a caucus of members within the union
to challenge the current leadership.[2]

Rosie's stress and the mention of her weekend work responsibilities are reminders of the extra hours that teachers regularly put in to do things like review student work and plan lessons. Place on top of this demanding profession the challenging responsibilities that teacher activists like Rosie take on and one can easily understand why she feels overwhelmed. She adds, "It's just a process, the fight continues. It's just like a constant struggle of trying to keep yourself clear enough to see the truth. To continue to listen to people and not get so stubborn and trying to get people to not fight over the petty stuff and trying to ground yourself and not get so tired that you can't focus or be clear." Rosie draws emotional parallels between her work in the classroom and her activism outside of the school walls: "Whether I'm in my classroom and I'm so stressed out or too tired or whatever and I snap or I start a fight that I shouldn't be fighting because I'm just so frustrated with the kids and the world or trying to organize something that doesn't work, it's just a matter of reconnecting, and I think the most important thing out of all of this, we need to find a way to support each other and to learn from each other and to grow together and not to judge each other."

Part IV: Empowering Students

Rosie draws clear parallels between her training as an organizer and her pedagogy as a teacher. Explaining her approach to teaching, Rosie says:

> I look at education in the same way I look at organizing. And I think good teaching is when you can assess where your student is at, or the person you're talking with, and kind of find their issues, find what they're passionate about, and meet them where they're at. Whether it's the content or with scaffolding [...] [good teaching is] finding their needs and what they're passionate about and then sculpting your lesson plan, your conversation, your content, from where they're at. And then also seeing the places where you can move them, where movement is possible and where they can grow as a student. And then also just giving them little tasks that they can achieve to make them feel good, but also pushing them, to make it rigorous or to push them to where they need to go to succeed. But not overwhelming them, so that they have no self-esteem left, and they're totally drowned in content, that they just feel bad about themselves.

This approach to teaching, both complex and comprehensive, can be seen when observing Rosie's classroom. Whether teaching students about the modern-day parallels between the themes in the *Grapes of Wrath* and present-day farm workers' struggles in the tomato picking industry, or creating space safe enough to challenge students to address controversial issues of gender identity, Rosie's organizing experience shapes her teaching pedagogy. For her unit on race and stereotypes, Rosie's approach is no different.

By the 2011 spring semester, Rosie has retired the pushcart she used in the beginning of the year to transport her teaching materials and is now assigned to teach in her own classroom after the neighboring small school allowed IHSPS to borrow the room. In this semipermanent space, Rosie is able to hang up student work, posters, and notes. The poster at the front of the room above her desk reads, "History is an argument about the past" and poses the question "How do we know what we know about the past?" Student work from both her social studies and English classes covers the majority of wall space. One set of student-made posters generated from the current unit explore the issues of race, stereotypes, and discrimination. The titles of the posters describe some of the topics the class has already explored: "Illusion of Race," "Christopher Columbus," "Rise of Race," "Where does the idea of race come from?" "Segregation in the United States," and "The Invention of Race." They all depict different scenes and moments in U.S. history when race was used to discriminate against a group of people—primarily African Americans and Native Americans.

It is the last period of the day on a Friday in May. With the end of the school year in sight and a beautiful spring day beckoning the weekend to come as soon as possible by spraying bright rays of sunshine through the tall classroom windows, Rosie's task is to prepare a roomful of 21 seniors just over a month away from graduation for their final social studies research essays. Just like all of her classes at IHSPS, the demographic make-up of the class is diverse with students reflecting African, Latino, Asian, and Arab backgrounds. For the first time in Rosie's classes, I notice two White students, whose families recently emigrated from Poland. Student chatter is lively at the start of class. Rosie moves to the dry-erase board at the front of the room and writes down the day's agenda:

> Do Now: Share your homework
>   1. Irish stereotypes
>   2. Choosing a topic
>   3. Research
> Homework: Front page of research

Before introducing her students to the research assignment, Rosie leads the class in finishing up their exploration of Irish stereotypes, mirroring how the class has previously learned about stereotypes and discrimination faced by other racial and ethnic groups in the United States.

For the "Do Now," students take out their homework and begin looking at it with their neighbors. The two-sided homework handout has political cartoons from the late 1800s depicting stereotypes of Irish Americans. Their homework assignment was to simply review the cartoons and come to class being ready to discuss their observations. The first is an 1876 Harper's Weekly cartoon of an Irish male sitting opposite a Black male on either side of an evenly balanced scale measuring their relative ignorance as new voting blocs in the North and South during the Reconstruction Era; the second, titled "St. Patrick's Day, 1867," illustrates a scene of drunken, rioting Irishmen viciously beating police officers with the words "RUM" and "BLOOD" prominently inscribed in the bottom corners of the cartoon panel.

After a few minutes of one-to-one sharing, Rosie opens up a full class discussion by asking students to identify how the Irish characters in the cartoons are being depicted. The students, adept at picking up on the details of the illustrations in the cartoons, call out their responses one by one.

"Violent."
"Drunk."
"Ugly."
"Apelike."
"Animalistic."
"Dirty."
"Wild."
"Out of control."
"Stupid."

Rosie writes these answers on the board and it is soon full of a list of negative Irish stereotypes apparent in the cartoons. After the students are finished sharing their observations, they copy down the list of stereotypes and Rosie hands out a summary of the class research essay assignment.

Rosie explains that the research essays will focus on answering one central research question: "How has the concept of race been used to marginalize various groups throughout American history and keep other groups in power?" The research question for the assignment is designed to push students to choose a racial or ethnic group and more deeply consider the impact and functionality of the stereotypes it faced at different points in U.S. history.

Rosie reads a list of groups, in addition to Irish Americans, that they have studied over the past two weeks: Native Americans, Chinese Americans, Jewish Americans, African Americans, and Mexican Americans. She adds that students may also approach her with ideas to explore different groups if they would like.

It strikes me that this unit is being taught to a group of students whose own personal and family histories in the United States span just the past few years. I wonder how much personal connection students make to these topics. For example, do African immigrant students see the historical discrimination against African Americans as relevant to their present-day experiences? As if sensing my own ponderings, two Polish students call over to Rosie and ask her if they can research stereotypes and discrimination experienced by Polish Americans. Rosie approves. I think about Rosie's own pedagogical principle of "finding [students'] needs and what they're passionate about and then sculpting your lesson plan, your conversation, your content, from where they're at." This research assignment makes these accommodations easily. By giving students multiple points of entry into the assignment, allowing them to choose a research focus in which they have personal interest, Rosie constructs a learning environment that is responsive to student interest.

After all her students have chosen a racial or ethnic group to focus on, Rosie writes the word "POWER" on the board at the front of the classroom. "The definition of being marginalized," Rosie says, "is being pushed away from power." She circles the word "POWER" and draws four arrows emanating outward from each side of the word, pointing and pushing toward the margins. At the end of these arrows, she explains, marginalized from "POWER" is where African Americans, Irish Americans, Chinese Americans, Native Americans, Jewish Americans, and Mexican Americans—and many others—have been forced to reside at different points across U.S. history. Her students nod as they recreate the diagram in their notebooks.

While on one level, the assignment is constructed to meet students where they are, it also pushes students to consider and understand the histories and experiences of oppressed groups through the concepts of "power" and "marginalization." Instructionally, connecting the historical functions of power and marginalization stands in contrast to a more traditional approach, which might merely ask students to document and describe examples of stereotypes and discrimination. The critical research question frames the assignment so that students must consider the intentionality and agenda behind social prejudice. It is this key framing of Rosie's class assignment that moves it from being simply meeting students where they are at to challenging students to grow by "seeing the places where you can move them, where movement is possible."

A month later, I make my final visit to Rosie's school. The 12th-grade teaching team has been working with Radio Rootz, a school program related to the radio journalism class Rosie took earlier in the year. Luckily, my visit includes the Radio Rootz listening party at which student groups will be airing their final radio journalism productions. We make our way to a large double-size classroom space used for dance classes where teachers and students are frantically setting up chairs to accommodate everyone expected to attend the listening party.

Students come in animated, loud, and full of nervous energy. It is a hot day outside and even though there are some fans going and the shades are drawn to keep the direct sunlight out, it is going to get steamy with nearly 75 of us crowded into one room. As the room warms up, people begin fanning themselves with their folders, books, and pieces of paper. The Radio Rootz instructors are huddled on the side, preparing for their presentation of the student-produced radio broadcasts, then move to the front, ready to get started.

The program is simple. A representative from each of the 12 groups of seniors introduces each piece, explaining the topic for the production that everyone is about to hear. The students are excited to hear themselves over the air and, as their voices are recognized, playful shoutouts to classmates are met with embarrassed squeals of laughter. The student production teams chose their own topics and the pieces present youthful perspectives on a wide variety of subjects: violence and safety, Islamophobia, teen sexual health, immigrant students and college access, dropping out of high school, wasting food, what NYC would be like without immigrants, the state of journalism and jobs, recycling, and the growth of technology.

For the broadcasts addressing neighborhood violence and Islamophobia, students include interviews with the IHSPS principal. In both instances, the principal draws a distinction between experiences with the community "inside" the school and what students face in the community "outside" the school. With respect to both the threat of physical violence and Islamophobic discrimination, the principal says, "We are a safe space in school, but outside is a different story." She frames the school as sanctuary. Indeed, the broadcasts uncover student stories of being targeted in stores and subways and getting robbed. Muslim students report being forced to endure ignorant comments made by strangers directed at them and their faith. All the broadcasts discuss the need for change.

I think about Rosie's focus on safe space in her classroom and her discussions of power with her students. If schools are really going to serve as "the hub of a community" and "work to bring communities together" as Rosie has told me, then functioning as safe space sanctuaries is not enough. Alone, they are just placeholders, isolated zones where students can learn and teachers can teach. Unless they are also activist spaces empowering students and teachers to influence community change, their potential power will be squandered. The Radio Rootz projects work to leverage the sanctuary of IHSPS to empower students to explore community issues with the expressed aim of influencing change. The students' stories help me understand what Rosie means when she says that social change work has "to be done on a political scale. It's more than what happens in the classroom, but yet it is everything that happens in the classroom."

The listening party comes to an end and the Radio Rootz instructors close by telling the students that some of their pieces were the best they have ever heard from high school students and announce that one or two will be aired on a local radio station. Rosie's smile beams with pride. I need to leave to catch my train home and head across the room to say goodbye. In this last moment of data collection, I feel emotional. Not wanting to leave or say farewell to Rosie, I smile and wish her luck for the last few weeks of what was an incredibly busy school year. I remember something she told me the day before: "I think right now I'm just so overwhelmed with everything I'm just thinking of the beginning. The best part about being a teacher is that every year you get to start off new." I hope that the summer months offer Rosie an opportunity for renewal because I know that it is important for the rest of us that she comes back each school year refreshed for her new start.

Part V: Reflections on Creating Space

Rosie's political development led her to understand the importance of space beyond its safety. In the Black feminist tradition, safe spaces have formed as prime locations for "resisting objectification as the Other" reflecting the "dialectical nature of oppression and activism" (Collins, 2009, p. 111). Rosie's portrait helps us understand that spaces need to be cultivated to be activist and empowering as well. By infusing the safe spaces she works hard to create with activist elements, Rosie is intent on empowering students and teachers who have been pushed to the margins of power to effect social justice change.

Critical theorists and researchers explore the politics of space by grappling with how the power relations that make up the various spaces occupying our lives inscribe themselves in our bodies, our actions, and our beings. Schools, in particular, are theorized as spaces that function to maintain and perpetuate power relations, and thus classrooms are inscribed with expectations about how the people in them should function with the teacher as the power figure and students as subordinates. However, spaces can also be disrupted and reformed to challenge dominant power relations. Radical education theorists have long proposed that schools should be seen as "democratic public spheres [...] to educate a citizenry capable of building a critical democracy" (Giroux & McLaren, 1986, p. 224) and teachers recast as "transformative intellectuals [who] treat students as critical agents, question how knowledge is produced and distributed, utilize dialogue, and make knowledge meaningful, critical, and ultimately emancipatory" (Giroux & McLaren, 1986, p. 215).

Consider what makes Rosie's classroom a radical space. It is radical because Rosie teaches about things that students likely will not learn anywhere else; because it deviates from the mainstream curricular script so dramatically; and because, at its root, Rosie's classroom is about creating a safe space within which students actively engage in an exploration of power. She invites and encourages critical thought, discomfort, and exploration and creates a space where it is safe to do so. Rosie's commitment to teaching students about power and marginalization mirrors the importance of these concepts in her own political development. Her experience as an LGBTQ student leader in college solidified for Rosie her visceral feelings from being marginalized and discriminated against. Then, as Rosie was being trained as an organizer, she found support in an activist space that deepened her understanding of power and powerlessness. As exhibited in her own life, feeling disempowered and marginalized was overcome through the creation of safe spaces within which she felt empowered and recognized. Rosie's classroom teaching is designed to provide a similar experience for her students who have marginalized identities as immigrants, youth of color, low-income, or nonnative English speakers.

However, most teachers probably do not enter the profession to "be an activist first" like Rosie did and Rosie's work with teachers is aimed at creating spaces for their own activist learning and development. Rosie's work with NYQueer mirrors her activist development at La Salle as she strove to make her college campus a safer space for LGBTQ students. Her focus on building teacher power through the union reflects her time and training as an organizer with SEIU. These spaces, in Rosie's case facilitated by activist groups like NYCoRE, TU, and GEM, are necessary for teachers to be able to be effective activists inside and outside of their classrooms. Whether for teachers or students, Rosie's work makes it clear that it is important to create space for people to fight for justice.

Notes

1. On a more hopeful note, in 2013, IHSPH teachers worked collectively to establish the International Dreamers Scholarship Fund to support graduates who are undocumented to afford attending college. In May 2014, the teachers at IHSPH successfully organized to boycott the administration of a citywide test at their school because they believed it was discriminatory against English Language Learners. Rosie was a key leader and contributor to both these efforts.
2. In large part, stemming from the work of "Voltron" the Movement of Rank and File Educators (MORE) has since formed, which is a social justice caucus of the UFT.

References

Collins, P.H. (2009). *Black feminist thought: Knowledge, consciousness, and the politics of empowerment*. New York: Routledge Classics.

Giroux, H.A. & McLaren, P. (1986). Teacher education and the politics of engagement: The case for democratic schooling. *Harvard Educational Review*, 56(3), 213–238.

Peterson, B. & Charney, M. (eds). (1999). *Transforming teacher unions: Fighting for better schools and social justice*. Milwaukee, WI: Rethinking Schools.

NATALIA ORTIZ: GROWING CONSCIOUSNESS AND COMMUNITY

Part I: Care and Consciousness

Natalia Ortiz lets out an embarrassed, but playful, laugh when she admits, "Oh God, when I was seven, I was the 'Queen of Puerto Rico.' I don't know if I told you that, but it was a New York pageant. It was crazy, my mom wanted me to be this superstar kid. So I won the contest for the little 'Queen of Puerto Rico.'" At the Queen of Puerto Rico pageant, Natalia had to talk about what she wanted to be when she grew up. "I picked out teacher," she recalls, "which is what I really wanted to be." She "wanted to make all students from different cultures feel comfortable." Raised by her mother, an immigrant from Chile, Natalia developed "this whole awareness of language and difficulties of what it meant to not be whatever it meant to be American," and has always wanted to "assist folks with whatever clash they're experiencing." Natalia attributes her sensitivity to cultural difference to her upbringing in an immigrant family and to the diverse set of friends she had growing up in New York. "I experienced it or saw my mom go through it," she says.

For instance, Natalia would often get frustrated at the supermarket when a cashier did not understand whatever her mother was saying. Natalia would help translate for her mother, but people "would get very short and impatient."

"Why are people so mean?" Natalia asked her mother. "When you're Latina, and you're a woman, you gotta fight. It's not gonna be easy, Natalia," her mother answered. As much as this was an early lesson in what it meant to be Latina, a woman, and to speak a language other than English, Natalia learned to "always try to be nice because I knew what Mom went through."

Natalia's recollections of her childhood are littered with moments of her early interest in teaching as a way to help and care for others. She has fond memories of second grade, when she would read books to kindergartners during lunch. "I've just always loved interacting with people, and I like to help," Natalia explains about her excitement to serve as a "reading teacher" for younger children. "In elementary school, I was the known helper, translator," Natalia remembers. When new Spanish-speaking students came to her school, Natalia's teachers told her, "Natalia, this is your buddy. You're in charge of helping the buddy." She would sit with them at lunch and translate and help the new students with their transitions into the school. "I enjoyed it," Natalia says. Then, for emphasis, she adds, "I loved it."

She has positive memories of many of her teachers as she was growing up. In elementary school, Natalia "had teachers who really cared" about her. She remembers struggling in elementary school when her parents decided to get a divorce and even crying at times. Her teachers were always there to comfort her and show their support. In high school, Natalia's favorite teacher was an English teacher she had for two different years, Ms. Porter. "She pushed me," Natalia says to explain why Ms. Porter was her favorite; she was both "cool" and "mean." Ms. Porter was smart, she "knew a lot," and "wore all these funky outfits." Students found her cool, but also knew that they "couldn't be too buddy buddy" with her. She was mean in that she was demanding of her students. Natalia remembers that because she was a good student, "teachers, for the most part, liked me." While others might let things slide because she was a good student, Ms. Porter would keep Natalia after school to work on her grammar and writing, an area Natalia "always struggled with." With her childhood interest in becoming a teacher reinforced by positive memories of grade school, Natalia started on her path toward the teaching profession with wide-eyed enthusiasm. She was ready to help students like she was helped, care for them as she was cared for, and generally give back to schools what she was fortunate enough to get out of them.

Years later, Natalia did indeed become a teacher and I sit in the back corner of her classroom at West Brooklyn Community High School (WBCHS) in a chair next to her teacher's desk. WBCHS is a small New York City high school, serving approximately 180 students, located in an old Catholic school building just a few blocks from the Fort Hamilton Parkway stop on the D train. She started teaching there when the school opened in 2006. It is a transfer school, which means that WBCHS students are "overage and undercredited." Perhaps they used to be truant, or were once incarcerated in juvenile detention, or maybe traditional high school just was not working out, or they decided to change their minds about dropping out; whatever the reason, the students at WBCHS have fewer credits than average peers their age. There are a few transfer schools throughout the city serving this particular student population to help them get the credits and pass the tests they need in order to earn a high school diploma. Among the transfer schools, WBCHS has a strong reputation, and from my conversations with Natalia, I know that she enjoys teaching there.

Students begin streaming into the classroom. One noticeable area is the corner of the room where I sit near Natalia's desk, which is located straight across from the entryway. Mixed in with memos, official school forms, and the New York City public school calendar, which hang from magnetic clips stuck to the chalkboard behind her desk, are posters, pictures, and other items hung on display. Natalia's values of diversity, respect, and justice are expressed through the posters—one about Mexican painter Frida Kahlo, another about Puerto Rican sovereignty, one from GLSEN (the Gay, Lesbian, and Straight Education Network), and another about children's rights. There are pictures and postcards propped up along the edge of the tray at the bottom of the chalkboard, including one that declares "Love your hood," a colorful, artistic, four-panel screen print of the word "Love," and another that has a picture of instructions to "Make your own revolution" out of unity, tears, love, and pride. There is a picture of Natalia with students at the New York AIDS Walk in 2011, an event she takes a group of students to each year, and the back of her chair is draped with a T-shirt that says "The Struggle Continues…"

Natalia, who stands just over five feet tall with an athletic frame built from her childhood of keeping up on the playing fields with her twin brother, has positioned herself near the doorway. Here, she can finish writing the lesson's objective, Do Now, and homework on the dry-erase board and still easily shift over to greet each arriving student with a firm handshake. The handshakes are noticeable because Natalia makes a point to do it with every student and, evident from the ease with which students offer their hands upon entry, it is clearly an expected routine in her classroom. The bounce of her thick, dark-brown curly hair bobbing up and down just short of her shoulders as she jumps back and forth between the board and the doorway reinforces Natalia's reputation for being full of energy. Write a few words, shake a student's hand. Write a few more words, shake another student's hand. "I love it, yes," Natalia shares about her handshaking routine. "Ever since I started the first year. I don't know how, but it's something I've done every year and every year it works wonders."

On the first day of school, Natalia breaks the ice with her students by telling them about her childhood to help them understand why she asks students to shake her hand every day. Natalia has very dry skin, so much so that her hands can be strewn with cracks. When she was little, other kids did not want to hold her hand at school and Natalia became very self-conscious. She tells her students that asking them to shake hands everyday helps her "get over it, but a lot of it is also out of respect." For Natalia, respect is central to her teaching, and it starts with students entering her classroom with this daily routine. Handshaking gives Natalia and her students the opportunity to connect with each other immediately as class begins. They get to start off by saying "Good morning, I recognize you, you see me." Right away, she gets a sense of how they are doing, whether they might feel sick, be in a bad mood, or have some other mental or emotional state that might impact their work in the classroom. At the end of class, they repeat the same routine. Natalia stands by the exit and, one by one, students shake her hand as they leave. "It's also an opportunity for me to say, 'You did a great job today,' 'Good job, keep it up,' or to say 'You're talking too much, you need to check that,' whatever. So we check in, we check out," Natalia explains. The routine is so ingrained that students will hold Natalia accountable, reminding her, "Miss, you didn't give me a handshake," in the rare moments when she might forget or be otherwise distracted at the start or end of class. All at once, Natalia's daily handshakes with her students establish feelings of mutual care and respect, provide opportunities to ensure at least a short moment of one-to-one connection, and reclaim Natalia's personal history as a school child for whom hand-to-hand contact produced anxiety and stress.

In addition to Natalia's caring sensibilities, she developed a consciousness about difference and power that informs her teaching. Her family upbringing taught her what it was like to adjust to new cultures and different surroundings; this not only positioned her well to play the helper-translator role for her new peers but also taught her early lessons about cultural difference. It was important to her mother that Natalia grow up speaking Spanish and Natalia learned Spanish first because, as her mother put it, "You're gonna learn

English in kindergarten anyway." Natalia and her twin brother also spent many of their childhood summers in Chile living with their aunts, uncles, and cousins. She remembers, "My mom sent us to Chile every summer when she could—because she wanted us to be bilingual, she also wanted us to know our family—instead of paying for summer camp, or just letting us hang around at home and not doing anything."

Summer in New York City is at the same time as winter in Chile, so when Natalia visited her cousins she would attend school with them. This schedule meant year-round schooling for Natalia during the years she visited her family abroad. Natalia did not always look forward to more school, but "in the end had a lot of fun in Chile anyway because the culture's so different." The "two realities" of Natalia's childhood—New York and Chile—built a sense "of trying to understand folks for their differences." Learning how her cousins lived in Chile presented her with an alternative to the ways things were done in New York. "I couldn't judge my family and I knew that they were living differently than me, but I wasn't sure how to interpret that. But I knew I couldn't get angry with them cuz they did some things differently," reflects Natalia. "You know, so it's cool if you tell me a story about what they do in another country, I'm like, oh, I understand."

With her own bicultural family as a reference point, Natalia embraced a diverse set of friends. "I feel like I was aware of differences from very early on," Natalia remembers as she names her best friends who were Tibetan, Pakistani, and Puerto Rican. "I went to how many Bar and Bat Mitzvahs, even though obviously I'm not Jewish," she laughs. "New York opened me up to those differences, the cultural awareness that maybe others don't have access to as easily as I did." In middle school, Natalia's best friend was a Tibetan girl who was born in India. Natalia visited her friend's house "all the time" in Astoria, Queens. Her friend's family was Buddhist and on Natalia's first visit she remembers seeing a picture of "the Dalai Lama hanging on the wall." Natalia thought, "it's beautiful," and, curious, she looked at her friend and pointed at the picture, asking, "Who's that?" "Oh, Natalia, you can't point," her friend responded. Instead, Natalia learned that when approaching or gesturing toward the Dalai Lama, you should have your hand open and palm out. Growing up with friends whose families were from other countries also meant that Natalia understood the pressures they felt "to blend into American culture and how difficult that was."

As Natalia developed her sensitivity to difference, her beliefs would sometimes clash with those of her peers, providing challenging moments of adolescent tension and discord. "I remember in ninth grade," Natalia starts, "my friend, Desiree, she was a very religious Christian, and we walked by a club that's in an old church in Manhattan." Desiree said, "Oh, my God, they're gonna go to hell," when she saw that there were people who were partying and drinking in what used to be a church. Then, Natalia and Desiree saw "right out in front there were two dudes making out" and Desiree "yelled out something about them going to hell." Natalia was mortified and embarrassed by Desiree's yelling and told her to stop. They ended up stopping on the sidewalk by a fire hydrant to debate Desiree's religious beliefs and Natalia's defense of gay people. When Desiree brought up what the Bible says about gay people, Natalia remembers saying, "OK, Des, the Bible also says you need to treat your neighbor like your-self, and the Bible also says you need to love all people for who they are. And so you're contradicting yourself. Cuz here you are saying these people, because they're gay, they're gonna go to hell. And you're treating them like crap, you're yelling at them, you're telling them that they're gonna go to hell, and that's horrible. If you call yourself a Christian woman, then you should really check how you're treating people." To this day, Natalia thinks that her sidewalk debate with Desiree may have changed her friend's feelings toward gay people.

Natalia's early lessons in difference served as a political primer for the more explicit consciousness she developed in college. If her desire to teach as a way to care for others was cultivated throughout grade school, then Natalia's political purpose for teaching was developed during her years at Wesleyan University. "I love Wesleyan," Natalia affectionately recalls about her time in college. "I'm thankful for Wes, because I think Wes politicized me, and taught me to think outside the box. Really, I'm sure my life experiences already were in me, but I think Wes gave me the language to express that." Natalia's learning in college helped her make sense of many of her life experiences. "I think it all started at Wes," Natalia says about her political analysis. "And it would have to be with my conversations with people, with peers, where I felt like, where the hell have I been? Why don't I know all this? Or, wow, y'all take things to a deeper level that I never thought about. I think that's when I started to really start thinking about how I've been socialized to think or believe, you know what I wore, how I thought, stuff like that. [...] I felt that I needed to do a lot of catching up."

Many of her classes and late-night discussions with her friends led to "Aaaaaah!" moments, "revelations" about the meaning and implications behind much of her experience growing up as a person of color in the United States. When our own conversation shifts to discussing her college experi-ences, Natalia starts to name some of the new concepts she was being exposed to: "institutionalized racism," "internalized racism," "systems of oppression," and "White privilege." Though I attended a different institution, it seems that Natalia and I share some similar politicizing college experiences. During college was also the first time I learned about these concepts of how power and privilege are constructed in our society. I also remember the enthusiasm and zeal with which I thrust myself into campus activities and activism centered on issues of race and racism. Having not had the opportunity to explore or even the exposure to these ideas in secondary school, college was a training ground for activist work as a person of color.

One specific classroom exchange sticks out clearly in Natalia's memory, when her "Cultural Psychology" professor challenged statements by two different students, one a male of color, the other a White male. When the student of color was challenged on three consecutive points, the student relented and said, "Oh, you're right, I'm sorry." In contrast, when the professor challenged the White male student, a White female student came to his defense by saying, "Well, I think you just misinterpreted him." Immediately, the professor pointed out to the class that no one tried to speak on behalf of the student of color, but as soon as a White male student was challenged, a classmate rose to his defense. His open and direct style made many students feel uncomfortable, especially those with privilege, but Natalia reflects that "at least there was a professor who was even pushing to think in that way [...]. For me, it was like, whoa, I need to really keep my eyes open more, because I never thought of this before or I never even realized it."

The eye-opening experiences in college manifested in Natalia's relationship with her mother. Exposure to new ways of thinking and new frames for understanding power, privilege, and oppression gave Natalia a set of tools to recognize things she felt were unjust. She started to put words to some of the political differences she felt she had with her mother. "I could stand up to Mom now," Natalia says, "and tell her things that I don't think are fair." When she was younger, there were things that Natalia felt were unfair or unjust, but she says, "I just didn't have the vocabulary, the language, or the confidence to stand up to my mom. Especially because my mom is my role model, I can't question my mom [...] and then I realized it's not necessarily getting angry at my mom, or bashing her beliefs, but it's definitely politicizing and educating my mom."

Because of their close relationship, disagreeing with her mother was not easy for Natalia. In 1978, Natalia's mother immigrated to the United States from Chile at the age of 21. She married Natalia's father, who was from Puerto

Rico, in 1981 and, almost two years later, Natalia and her twin brother were born. Natalia spent the first seven years of her life with her mother, father, and brother in an apartment in midtown Manhattan, near the United Nations, where her father was a building super, which meant they had a rent-free apartment. Her parents' relationship was not healthy, but according to Natalia, her mother was "at first, really dependent" on her father because when "she came here from Chile, she didn't know the language well, was kind of living off my dad and taking care of her two kids."

By the time Natalia and her brother were seven years old, her mother was working in New York for Codelco, a Chilean copper mining company, where she could both speak Spanish and learn English. At this point, Natalia says her mother "finally felt safe enough to pick up and go and leave my dad." They lived with her mother's friend for about three months before they were able to get a subsidized apartment on Roosevelt Island, a small island dotted with apartment buildings nestled in the middle of the East River between Manhattan and Queens, where Natalia would live until she graduated from high school. Natalia says that overall "there were times obviously that were rough, especially with the whole Mom-Dad situation and the single parent thing. But I had a pretty strong mom to hold down the fort."

A lot of the disagreements between Natalia and her mother revolve around issues of race. When Natalia was young, her mother once told her that she should have Black friends, but never to date or marry a Black man. "I always knew it was wrong, but I never said anything about it," Natalia shakes her head. "It wasn't until recently when I told her, 'Maa, do you remember when you said that?'" Reflecting on it now, Natalia realizes that while growing up in Chile, her mother did not know any Black people and "the first time she encountered a Black person was when she was in high school, and a student visited from some country in Africa. They were playing a game and she didn't even want to hold his hand because she didn't know any better." Then, after moving to the United States, negative stereotypes about Black people were reinforced by the U.S. society, so she "never dealt with whatever '-isms' she had toward Black folks."

Natalia is hesitant to talk about her mother in this way. I can see that she is torn between this critical view and upholding her mother as a role model—a strong Latina who raised twins on her own in New York City, navigating the public education system and sending them both to a highly selective university. The sacrifices and hard work made by Natalia's mother and the unconditional love she has for her children make it difficult for Natalia to talk about any flaws. With scrunched eyebrows and nervous pauses during which

I imagine she thinks about how to frame the stories she tells, Natalia contin-ues to talk about how she challenges her mother's social and political beliefs.

Whether Natalia is critiquing her mother's assumption that when some-one was robbed in their community that it must have been done by a "a Black kid" or that Natalia's ex-boyfriend, a hip-hop artist with long braids and baggy clothes, must not have attended college, the exchanges often start out with Natalia pointing out, "Maa, seriously, that's racist." To which her mother replies, "For you, why does it always have to be about race, Natalia?" But, some of these conversations seem to be sinking in. Just recently, her mother had some girlfriends over the house and they were talking about their friend's new puppy, Coco Blanco.

"Why didn't you get a black dog?" one friend asked.

"Oh well, you know, white is better," another added with a laugh.

Natalia's mother responded, "You have to be careful with comments like that, especially around Natalia."

Natalia smiles and sighs when telling this part of the story. "I would have liked it and preferred if she said, 'You need to not make that comment,' and just left it at that." As much as it has been difficult to challenge her mother, these discussions and debates have deepened their relationship. Sharing these difficult conversations with her mother ensures that Natalia engages in their relation-ship as her full self. Like when Natalia shakes hands with her students, when she and her mother engage in these important exchanges about race and politics, they can say to each other, "I recognize you, you see me." The love and respect they have as mother and daughter endures through critical disagreement.

For all of her accomplishments, Natalia's teaching and activism find their roots in these personal moments of challenge. Whether it is her own beliefs and assumptions being challenged by new perspectives and experiences, or the challenges she poses to her friends and family based on her sense of justice, the development of Natalia's political consciousness set the stage for her more public manifestations of teacher activism.

Part II: Planting Seeds

A consistent theme in Natalia's U.S. history and government classes is an explo-ration of "winners and losers" and contrasting "moving upward or forward" with "someone always getting stepped on or pushed aside." She wants her students to learn about making the world a different and better place that no longer pushes people aside, but that instead sees and recognizes everyone's humanity. This theme is perhaps why Natalia seems to revel in teaching about the Industrial and Progressive Eras, both prominent portions of the New York State U.S. History Regents curriculum rich with historical examples contrasting wealth and poverty, power and pushback. During a visit to Natalia's U.S. History II class, she is wrapping up a unit on the Industrial Period of the late 19th and early 20th centuries. It is a small class, like most at WBCHS, with only 16 students on the register. Today, only ten students are present. When students enter the room, they shake hands with Natalia, sit down, and take out their notebooks. They look toward the board to write down the "Do Now," which asks students whether they agree or disagree with the following statement: "The wealth of a few people masks society's problems, including politics and poverty."

Natalia opens up discussion about the statement. All the students agree with it and relate it to government corruption and cover-ups. Some bring up conspiracy theories about 9/11, and how the government used 9/11 as an excuse to go to war. They also talk about how the media portrays America as a place of wealth and celebrity, distracting people from reality. "The quote is basically an expression of what capitalism is all about," concludes one student in a statement that serves to sum up their collective assessment of the quotation.

"Do any of you disagree with the quote?" Natalia asks. "Come on, step up and be bold. Disagree with the rest of the class!" No one does, and so Natalia moves on to ask students what they think should be done about the corruption they are describing: "If you all agree that the U.S. is covering up poverty and problems in society, what should we do about it?"

"Protest," a student responds.

"OK, who's willing to do that?" Natalia asks.

"Nah, I don't want to stand outside all day," another student answers.

"We've got better things to do," another adds, while her neighbor wonders, "Would it actually make a difference?"

"I give change to homeless people on the street," declares the student who said he did not want to stand outside all day.

Natalia asks the class if they think giving away spare change makes a difference and their conversation shifts to society's general attitudes toward poor people and poverty. It is a brief, but lively exchange and ends when one student talks about how students' attitudes are to laugh at the poor. "Think about how judgmental we are about people's shoes and clothes, hairdos, etc.," she says. "We laugh at the poor everyday. We just don't realize it—it's a capitalist mentality."

This opening conversation lasts about ten minutes before Natalia takes the opportunity to transition into the day's history lesson about the Gilded Age. The Do Now statement was a quotation taken from the Industrial Era when increasing riches, represented by the glitz and glamour of wealthy industrialists, masked the abject poverty that was the stark reality for many workers and everyday people. Natalia gives a mini lecture about the Gilded Age and students take notes. Her lecture style is physically active. She moves in and out between the clusters of desks where students sit, paces back and forth when at the front of the room, and gestures with her hands frequently. She peppers students with quick questions. Why would people call it the Gilded Age? What is the shiny exterior covering up? How is this similar to today? Sometimes Natalia accepts answers as they are shouted out; for others, she tells students to raise their hands. Whenever students answer, she is quick to give high fives. The pace is quick and exciting, and all of the students participate by answering questions and taking notes.

Natalia presents her curriculum using a critical historical lens examining both "winners and losers" by balancing the celebration of increasing U.S. wealth and power during the Industrial Age with a substantive exploration of attitudes toward poverty. Then, not only does she raise the topic of how the celebration of the wealth of a few can mask the poverty-stricken realities of the many, she pushes students to consider what they can actually do about it. Pedagogically, this focus on potential action is a crucial step toward making her classroom emphasize more than learning about inequality and injustice; it is also about doing something and taking action against inequality and injustice.

It was not until Natalia attended college when she "realized students and children are agents of change." And even though she felt well supported in grade school, Natalia says, "I also think that what I learned at Wes, I should have learned in high school or even before then." Especially knowing that not all her students will have the opportunity to attend a college like Wesleyan, Natalia believes her classroom teaching should "do the best it can" to bring that intellectual experience to them. She focuses on developing students' critical thinking, "giving them the tools to question things and think about them differently." Natalia understands that her classroom alone will not be enough to replicate the political awakenings she had in college, but she hopes that for her students "the little seeds I'm planting can be developed."

"Teaching is revolutionary," Natalia says. "I'm preparing lesson plans, I'm working with children on their social and emotional development. The fact that I'm educating students about issues or things that maybe they've never learned or thought about and the fact that I'm teaching them how to think, I'm helping them find their voice. I'm helping them realize how important their voice is, and how they are human beings of this society, and that they shouldn't feel disempowered and that through the classroom we have power." Yet, as her student teaching experience in the Boston Public Schools taught her, an emphasis on planting seeds of political consciousness is not enough. As a graduate student in Harvard's Teacher Education Program, Natalia developed an understanding of the political imperative to explicitly focus on teaching academic skills to students who have been caught in urban public school systems that have historically failed them.

When Natalia entered into her graduate student teaching practicum, she "created a whole social justice unit, and it was all about the 1960s and all the movements, so like the Brown Berets, the Young Lords, Black Panthers, right. And about the inside and the outside approaches to reform and protest to change the system." She was excited to teach this unit, which included so much of what raised her own political consciousness and represented what she wished she had been exposed to before college. "I actually got a chance to teach a lot of it," Natalia says, but in the middle of the unit, her students were required to take a standardized literacy test. Natalia quickly realized that her students had "very low literacy skills," which was not the focus of her unit. "A lot of my focus was the content, knowing history," Natalia recalls. "And I guess I didn't focus on the skills or the critical thinking, or the literacy or the reading and writing. But at that moment, my definition of social justice changed. It's not just about what you teach, but how you teach and the skills you're incorporating into the content. Because if I can't help prepare a student how to write, or read, or analyze, I can talk at them all day long, but I'm not doing them any good at all. I'm only just hurting them." Now, Natalia's pedagogy integrates the cultivation of an action-oriented critical consciousness and academic skills. "It's not just me teaching them Malcolm X," Natalia says. "It's how to write, how to read, how to analyze, how to think."

One element of the New York State Regents U.S. History exams is their emphasis on important U.S. Supreme Court decisions. Multiple choice, document-based, and thematic essay questions are often in reference to these court cases, and Natalia builds her U.S. Government curriculum around them. I visit class on a day when students are preparing for their roles as either lawyers or justices for a mock trial based on the *Roe v. Wade* decision in 1973, establishing the high court's current legal precedent regarding abortion. A straightforward and simple Do Now is written on the board: "What is one question a justice can ask Jane Roe? And, one question to Wade?" There are only nine students in the class and they each sit down quickly to complete the Do Now. Just a few minutes into the class, Natalia asks for volunteers to share their questions for Roe and Wade. She writes them down in a T-chart on the chalkboard:

Jane Roe	D. A. Wade of Texas
o Isn't a fetus a life? Therefore, shouldn't it be protected by the 14th Amendment?	o Why are you against abortion?
o How is abortion an issue of privacy if a life is being taken away?	o Why do you feel it's your right to regulate medical practices?
o Isn't abortion just as bad as murder?	o Why are you invading women's privacy rights?

Based on the questions they share, the students demonstrate their understanding of the basic issues that were debated in *Roe v. Wade*. After reviewing the questions, Natalia gathers everyone's attention by announcing, "Drum roll, please!" Students rapidly bang their desks with their pens, pencils, or hands, while a few patter on the floor with their feet. Each student listens with anticipation as names are called and they are assigned "Justice," "Roe lawyer," or "Wade lawyer," representing the roles they will portray for the following day's mock trial. Next, the class breaks into three small groups according to their roles to prepare additional questions, write statements that would answer anticipated questions, and form the legal arguments they will need to represent their assigned perspectives.

As students do this work, Natalia moves back and forth between the small groups and helps them practice asking and answering the questions out loud based on what they have prepared. She challenges some of their points and helps groups refine their arguments, reminding them to look back at the Constitutional Amendments and clauses that are being brought into play and to refer to the packets they each have with the actual court opinions printed in them.

In less than an hour, the full range of Natalia's pedagogy is on display. Her approach to teaching Supreme Court decisions helps raise the level of critical consciousness in the classroom by working with students to see and analyze all sides of the arguments; students' leadership skills are put to the test as they will act out their roles as justices or lawyers, both roles that require agentic assertions of voice; and students work on their academic skills by writing statements and opinions based on the questions they brainstorm together. All of this happens while students are learning about content likely to show up on the state U.S. History Regents exam, which they are required to pass for graduation. Having taught about U.S. Supreme Court cases myself as a history teacher in the Bronx, I leave the class period impressed with the students' preparation to discuss the legal arguments and merits of the *Roe v. Wade* decision and convinced of Natalia's seed-planting abilities.

Part III: Developing Leaders

After Natalia's U.S. Government class ends, we sit together in the WBCHS staff lounge, which is a makeshift area of the school cafeteria sectioned off by office space dividers. "There's a new position in the school," Natalia says by way of an update on her extracurricular activities. "It's called the Youth Leadership Board advisor." The Youth Leadership Board (YLB) is "two years new" and it serves as a youth-led student organization that plans events and community projects after school hours. Natalia has been the staff support person for the YLB from the start and she says, "I love it because it's organizing students to do work outside of school." The YLB provides Natalia a direct outlet through which to help students to understand their own leadership potential and encourage them to become agents of change. It is an avenue for Natalia to work with students to take action around things they care about, an extension of the action-oriented conversations they have in her classroom. A major success for YLB in the past year was its recruitment of WBCHS students and staff to participate in the annual New York City AIDS Walk, an event organized by Gay Men's Health Crisis (GMHC) since 1986 to raise awareness and money to fight against the AIDS epidemic in the city. "We've been doing the AIDS Walk for three years now and the first year we had maybe 15 people show up," Natalia explains. "The second year we had 15 sign up, but only five showed up. This year, because the Youth Leadership Board organized it and the kids were hyping it up, we had 53 students sign up and 48 showed up." There is a prideful tone in her voice as she talks about the YLB leaders, almost as a mother might highlight the accomplishments of her children.

I arrive early at WBCHS one morning in early June to attend a YLB meeting. The meeting starts at eight a.m. and has a packed agenda: the annual student-staff basketball game, an upcoming field trip for graduating students, and follow-up activities related to a recent fundraiser for tsunami relief efforts in Japan.[1] Students facilitate the meeting, but Natalia plays an important advisory role. The students decide that they need to recruit more girls to play in the staff-student basketball game and discuss strategies to do so. They also decide to blow up and hang a thank you letter they received from the Japan Society for the school's tsunami relief donation. Finally, they delegate responsibilities for planning the graduation event, wanting to make sure that their graduating peers have a good time celebrating their accomplishment. Natalia does not contribute directly to the decision-making, but guides the students by emphasizing the ways they must act responsibly as leaders, including following through on their responsibilities and serving as positive role models in the school community. Her reminders stem from a recent flare-up within the YLB group. If Natalia's role is like a proud mother for the YLB, then the group as a whole acts like a small family—love and camaraderie mixed with disagreements and tension.

The most recent tensions were sparked by an incident on the way back from a youth leadership conference. As the YLB leaders were on the subway returning to Brooklyn, Natalia overheard one of them say, "That's so gay." She does not remember what the student was referring to, but she pushed back on the comment.

> "Did you just say, 'That's so gay'?" Natalia asked.
> "Yeah," responded the student.
> "Wow, why'd you say that?" Natalia continued.
> "Because he's whacked."
> "Alright, so why not use a word like whacked?"

An argument ensued between two male YLB students and Natalia and a female YLB leader, Gabrielle, who had recently come out to the group as queer. While the argument ranged from topics of freedom of speech, religious beliefs, how much control people have over their sexual preference, and YLB's own commitment to values of nondiscrimination, it ended with the students being upset. The boys were angry with Natalia for challenging them and Gabrielle was upset with the boys for offending her and making her feel uncomfortable. "All of a sudden, I felt like my family was breaking up," Natalia recalls. She explains that all of the students in YLB grow close to each other and they serve as each other's best friends and community at WBCHS. It was significant, then, that the tensions carried over into school the next day in Natalia's history class when one of the boys asked for his seat to be moved away from next to Gabrielle. After Natalia declined his request, he ended up cutting her class. On that Tuesday, there was a YLB meeting and Natalia had plans to talk about how the group needed to be able to have difficult conversations. Instead, Gabrielle approached Natalia and asked, "Miss, can you put me on the agenda because I have to talk to the YLB."

When it was her turn on the agenda, Gabrielle said, "I think as a Youth Leadership Board, we should talk about how people felt and what happened on Friday." She continued by explaining, "At home I don't feel accepted. And I feel like here at school I have a community that accepts me for who I am and YLB is an even closer community, it's like a family. So I felt hurt because I didn't feel accepted on Friday." Then, YLB members took turns sharing their feelings about what had happened on the subway ride, including Natalia. "One of the things that is always so amazing is when the students themselves bring up the issue without me having to push it," Natalia reflects. "Those are the moments where I'm, like, this is beautiful, because they've been able to create a little space where they all feel comfortable talking to each other and being honest with each other. And yeah, I've helped facilitate that." For Natalia, the leadership development of her students is tied directly to their own political consciousness. A focus on their ability to discuss and process the deeper social and political dynamics at play in their work and interpersonal relationships reflects Natalia's developmental experience in college and with her own family.

Natalia's leadership has continued to evolve since becoming a teacher. Much of her development is due to her involvement in so many different activities at her school and outside of it. However, even with everything that she does, Natalia reacts to being called a teacher activist: "I guess I would say I'm an activist, but I don't like to use that term freely." She outlines the ongoing tensions of being a teacher and activist, the competing demands for her time and energy, and the nagging sense that "I could do more, this isn't enough."

Sitting in her classroom in a rare free moment after school, Natalia runs through her weekly schedule of after-work commitments: Mondays—afterschool tutoring or NYCoRE meetings; Tuesdays—professional development (PD) or Instructional Leadership Team meetings; Wednesdays—afterschool tutoring and therapy; Thursdays—activist meetings; Fridays—"I don't have anything, thank God." Typically, by the time she is done for the day it is five, six, or even seven o'clock and Natalia is tired and just wants "to go home to Brooklyn." But sometimes there are meetings in Manhattan in the evening, in which case she does not get home until nine or ten o'clock. "And then you have to grade, then you have to plan," Natalia reflects. "I have to be careful with the choices I make if I want to continue to be a good teacher for my students." It is this last part of her statement that she drives home. As much as being an activist takes Natalia outside her classroom, she believes that her first priority must be her teaching.

"I've met some activists who—their heart is in activism, but their teaching isn't up to par," Natalia explains. "So it's kind of like their activism is jeopardizing their teaching, and that actually makes me—it angers me. Because I feel like, it's an injustice to our children." For her, part of being an effective teacher activist is striking the right balance between "giving as much as I can to activism," which Natalia takes to mean the activist work she does outside her classroom, and "making sure my kids are learning and that I'm not failing them as a teacher." All at once, Natalia feels overworked as a teacher and that she is not doing enough as an activist. Talking to her activist friends who are not teachers, she frequently has to tell them, "I'm sorry, I can't make it to your protest. I actually have to grade and I have to plan." And Natalia often feels guilty about not going to activist events, but at the same time, she recognizes the important role that her teaching plays in the overall social justice struggle. "I'm working with children, I'm working with the future. These people can be the next activists. You have to understand, what I'm trying to do is not not support you in this protest, but you need all avenues; you need me, just like I need you. I'm glad you're out there, but can you be glad for me that I'm in the classroom doing this?"

Nevertheless, mostly due to her involvement with NYCoRE, Natalia's activist life outside of her classroom is filled to the brim. Her introduction to NYCoRE came in 2004 as an undergraduate when she spent a semester in New York City working in a public high school and taking graduate-level education courses at Bank Street College. While she was in New York for the semester, the NYC Department of Education instituted a policy of basing third-grade promotion solely on student scores on citywide tests. There was an outcry from teachers, parents, and other community members against the new policy and Natalia attended a protest action organized by NYCoRE where teachers were speaking out against the policy at a Panel for Education Policy (PEP) meeting. "I was like, 'Oh, teachers can do this? Cool!'" Natalia remembers. "And so, it was like, OK, there's a cool group of teachers who actually care about what's going on with kids, and most of them don't even teach third-graders. That was my first exposure to NYCoRE."

When Natalia came back to NYC three years later as a full-time teacher, she sought out NYCoRE and joined the organization's email listserv. "I love the emails," Natalia smiles. "Whether it's free educational resources, or protests, or some fundraiser party or something, it's like, wow, I want to go to this, and this, and this. I could literally fill up my calendar with things I get on the NYCoRE listserv." But, the listserv is just the tip of the iceberg; as Natalia's teaching career has progressed, with each year her involvement with NYCoRE has increased. "It's a great medium," Natalia says about NYCoRE. "I'm able to be a teacher, but I'm also able to be active with them, and be part of the listserv and try to go to as many things as possible." Addressing the tension Natalia describes in balancing the demands of being a teacher and activist, NYCoRE has supported her to be both simultaneously.

Natalia describes NYCoRE as a "home base" and "support system." "Sometimes you feel alone," she states, invoking the feelings of isolation that many teacher activists often have. "It's good to have people who kind of think like you, who are trying to teach like you. And, you're like, phew, finally I can find a niche here in this city." Natalia's niche as a teacher activist and her deeper connections with NYCoRE have been largely carved out by the NYCoRE Inquiry to Action Groups (ItAGs)—teacher and community-led study groups that meet weekly for two months during the second half of the school year. They started in 2005 and have been a key avenue leading educators to get involved in NYCoRE.

"I've been doing ItAGs since I started teaching," says Natalia. "And for me, that's an avenue to keep my mind stimulated and to be connected to more than just my classroom. I started doing them because I need to talk to other educators, I need to see other activists, I need to learn how to include all of this in my classroom because I'm learning." Natalia's participation in ItAGs started as a participant in her first two years, which led to her being a facilitator in her third and fourth years. She has co-coordinated them since becoming part of the NYCoRE core leadership team in 2010. "I see it as a form of activism," Natalia explains. "I can always keep learning, and if I can help new teachers going into classrooms, and other teachers who want to do it, find ways to teach so that our kids are learning social justice issues or being exposed to ideas that they've never been exposed to, or going to marches or going to rallies, then I'm going to do that. If that's my vehicle, then that's what I'm going to do."

Natalia's ItAG participation has resulted in tangible changes in her classroom and school. The first ItAG she joined was focused on the "African Diaspora through Cultural Arts" and produced "a book of how to use the arts and explaining the Diaspora in our classrooms." Natalia immediately applied what she had learned to her classroom teaching. "I did a whole storytelling unit with my government class, where they had to create stories about the Supreme Court cases and tell them to the class through movement and sound. It was cool!" Natalia reflects. "And I never would have thought of that [without the ItAG]."

The next year, Natalia signed up for an ItAG focused on the work of Paulo Freire and Augusto Boal. She also recruited both her principal and assistant principal to join with her. Together, they studied excerpts from Freire's various writings about pedagogy and Boal's liberatory dramatic exercises and techniques known as "theater of the oppressed." Natalia implemented "a lot of Boal games" into her classroom and her school's leadership team restructured the way it did PD as a staff. Natalia, her principal, and assistant principal came back from their ItAG experience focused on "trying to implement community" for the staff and doing "physical activities and movement together." They integrated Boal's movement and theatrically oriented exercises into staff PD. "We do an opening activity with movement and, at the end, we have a closing, like make a sound that represents how you're feeling about today's PD," explains Natalia. "It has strengthened our PD, and every teacher has said, 'Wow, PD is great this year.' It's a lot better because the focus is about coming together as a community and we use movement and sound, not always talking or being talked at."

Natalia's positive experience with Boal-influenced activities at WBCHS has influenced how she exercises leadership in the NYCoRE community. Attending a NYCoRE member meeting in May 2011, I witness Natalia's facilitation of the group icebreaker. NYCoRE member meetings occur every first Friday in each month and they attract about 50 teachers and educators from across the city. Before delving into a political education session focused on the recent U.S. assassination of Osama Bin Laden and an anticipated rise in blatant Islamophobia and bullying of Muslim, Arab, and South Asian youth, Natalia's job is to facilitate an activity that will energize the Friday evening crowd. When it seems like most people have arrived, she introduces a sound and motion game called "Deejay."

Natalia asks everyone to stand in a circle. She is in the middle, constantly springing off her feet, turning her body in different directions and making eye contact all around the circle. She tells everyone to figure out a repetitive noise they can make with their mouths and bodies. When she points at a person, they need to make their noise. The goal is for the "deejay," who stands in the middle, to keep pointing at different people to make their noises as a way to blend everyone's sounds together to make "music." It is a fun game and everyone laughs at the creative noises people come up with—snorting, yelping, and growling noises, mixed with clapping, snapping, and stomping sounds.

Natalia serves as the first deejay to show everyone how the game works. As she is running around the circle cueing different people to make their noises, a coworker and friend of Natalia's whom I happen to be standing next to, says with wonder, "Where does she get that energy?!" Here, just as she does with her YLB students, Natalia leads by example. Yes, it is a Friday evening after a long, hard work week, but it is also time for NYCoRE members to come together and act collectively. Natalia's leadership emphasizes the importance of these collective moments as she works to help YLB be a family, her staff at WBCHS be a community, and NYCoRE members make music.

Part IV: Building Community

Natalia's increasing leadership role within NYCoRE has extended her involvement beyond ItAGs. As a person of color and someone who has developed an analysis of racial oppression since college, Natalia is looked to as an important leader for NYCoRE's efforts to more effectively engage teachers of color and to address issues of racial justice in education. A member of color recently shared with Natalia her concerns that member meetings are predominantly White. In particular, and this is true even in the core leadership, there are not many Black teachers who are involved in NYCoRE. Natalia notes that there are a number of ways to think about race when it comes to NYCoRE. She challenges the organization to consider the internal race issues: how the dynamics of race play out within NYCoRE as an organization by considering who the leadership is, how interactions between members are handled, and how many people of color are involved versus White people. Separately, there are also external race issues: how the work that NYCoRE does centrally addresses issues of race and the impact it has on racial justice.

One effort that Natalia and two other core leaders of color have initiated is a series of discussions being held for NYCoRE members of color. The effort is relatively new when we speak, but the first two meetings have encouraged Natalia. Members of color have stressed the important role that NYCoRE plays to help them find like-minded teachers and continue to learn how to be better teacher activists. Though many members highlighted the positive role that their relationships with other members of color have played in their commitment to NYCoRE, they expressed a desire for there to be more NYCoRE members who look like them. The lack of diversity in the general NYCoRE membership has manifested in some perceived tensions that Natalia has identified in her own lack of comfort and confidence discussing social justice union activism. The sense that White teacher activists dominate conversations about labor-oriented politics makes it difficult for teacher activists of color to gain access to these discussions.

Unions were "something that I really couldn't care less about," Natalia shares when thinking about her own reactions to NYCoRE's growing focus on teacher union issues. Yet, with the increasingly public attacks on teachers, Natalia recognizes the role of the teachers' union is central to the social justice struggle. It was not until she became more deeply involved with NYCoRE that she developed the language and understanding of social justice issues through a labor-oriented lens. "We're very much headed in the direction of neoliberalism, which is important to understand," Natalia shares. "But I think making the connection to race needs to be more concrete because it ends up really hurting our Black and Brown youth, through things like school closures and privatization." She wants to unpack what issues of race and racism have to do with neoliberal education reform strategies, such as school closures, privatization, and attacking unions and seniority rights.

Natalia compares her own upbringing—being raised by a single mother who immigrated to the United States and was not politically active—with one of her White colleagues whose parents were "very involved in political activism [...] and were also very involved with labor and unions." She concludes that she and others who similarly lack a labor-oriented political analysis need time and space to learn. "I experienced oppression and I experienced a bunch of things in high school," Natalia relates. "But I didn't have the vocabulary to talk about it until I went to Wesleyan [...]. We need to break down neoliberalism for people who don't have the language for it so it's tangible, because right now, it's here."

Natalia's commitment to helping others learn the language necessary to access the activist work of NYCoRE is reminiscent of her role as the designated "helper" and "translator" in grade school, but in this case it takes on a more political nature. She has realized that to sustain and further the work of teacher activists, it is necessary to continue to engage in political education to push teachers to gain deeper knowledge and analyses of the challenges facing public schools. Political education for NYCoRE members is important for members of color to feel more confident and connected to issues in which many White members already seemed well-versed, and for White members to deepen their analysis of race and racism as they work together in a multiracial collective.

Natalia's commitment to continuing her political education also extends beyond NYCoRE. The Venceremos Brigade (VB) started in 1969 to show solidarity with the Cuban Revolution by working side by side with Cuban workers and challenging U.S. policies toward Cuba. Each year, VB organizes a group of "brigadistas" to travel to Cuba in open opposition to and violation of U.S. government travel restrictions to the island. The trips include work, education, and sightseeing, and when they return to the United States, brigadistas proudly proclaim that they are coming back from Cuba when they arrive at U.S. Customs in a collective act of civil disobedience.

Natalia has participated in two VB trips. "I've always wanted to go to Cuba," she explains about her initial interest in VB. "Because I want to see what another system of government looks like, and a lot of it was also that I learned about the Spanish-Cuban-American War. I have to teach the Spanish-Cuban-American War. We talk about the Cold War, we talk about Castro, we talk about Cuba, so it's kind of, like, am I just feeding the same U.S. brainwashing about communism and Castro? I don't want to do that. But I also don't want to take the whole left side of the debate without really knowing what it is like in Cuba."

I attend a VB fundraiser with Natalia featuring a reportback from brigadistas who were part of the most recent trip. VB fundraisers seek to create community by connecting those who have traveled to Cuba with VB to those who have not gone but have a shared political interest in challenging U.S. policy toward Cuba. While I was growing up, my father was involved with solidarity work connecting activists in the United States to leftist community struggles in Central America. Throughout the 1980s, the U.S. government backed military dictatorships and right-wing resistance to popularly elected governments in countries like El Salvador, Nicaragua, and Guatemala. Similar to the brigadistas, the assumption for my father's activist community was that the best political education about what was really happening in Central America was for people to travel there in solidarity with the local communities fighting for progressive, social justice change and to return home to talk to others about what they saw and learned while they were there.

Upon arriving at the fundraiser, I am brought back to what these events are invariably like. There are the event organizers scrambling around to set up the food and drink tables, the poster and literature displays, the T-shirts for sale, and the slide show projector. Tonight, pictures are projected from a laptop also softly playing Cuban salsa and rumba music. Natalia is moving all around the room, and she seems to know most everybody. "Nataaalia!" people exclaim as she slides over to say hello. She dances with some, warmly embraces others, and greets everyone with a big smile.

As the hour approaches six p.m., the official start time, setup is complete and guests start to arrive in larger numbers. Quickly, the room fills with about 100 attendees, including four of Natalia's colleagues from WBCHS. As guests line up for food—a mix of homemade rice and beans, chicken, and stew—the room is abuzz. Music plays a little more loudly and people mingle throughout the space, making new connections and catching up with old friends. It is a family-friendly environment and toddlers are welcome and running about. In addition to the music, there are blinking Christmas tree lights wrapped around the big speakers at the front of the room. Streamers with Cuban and VB flags hang between the large columns, which surround the center area and demarcate the makeshift dance floor for later. The home-cooked meal adds to the feelings of family and community that preside over the festive atmosphere.

The program begins shortly after seven p.m. This evening, "brigadistas" from Delegation 41, which traveled in the summer of 2010, will be reporting back about their trip. They range from middle-age White women to a 16-year-old Latina high school student. The presenters touch upon various themes. One of the most striking is their commentary on political consciousness. While in Cuba, they found that average Cubans could generally talk about political issues with more nuance and depth than the average U.S. citizen. One speaker notes how this reality is a dangerous one for the U.S. government because the more U.S. citizens who see and understand "the real Cuba and real Cubans," then the more apt we are to be against our government's policies.

"I had to come back and completely change my PowerPoint about the Spanish-Cuban-American War," Natalia says, reflecting about her own experience returning from Cuba, armed with Cuban textbooks about the United States. "We're taught that Jose Marti deliberately bombed some of the sugar plantations so that the U.S. could get involved. When I brought that up, Cubans thought it was hilarious. They were, like, 'What? Jose Marti would never do that. In fact, Jose Marti didn't want the U.S. government to get involved.'"

Throughout the event, Natalia is busy working the media equipment. She makes sure that the volume is right, the music is playing, the pictures are showing, and the videos are rolling. She jokes with me toward the end of the night and says, "What are you going to write, 'She was on the floor messing with the computer all night?'" It is funny because this is really what she was primarily doing, but it is important to recognize that this, too, is the work of an activist. Her work is not about the obvious actions on public display, but it is in the details of how events like these are even possible. Without leaders like Natalia arriving early to set up, getting the slides together, choosing the musical play list, and more, then the event would lose its effect. Like in Natalia's classroom, the community being formed is as important to the political education as the content of the presentations. "Hugs, kisses, smiles, and squeals," I say to her. "That's what I'm going to write about what happens here." She and her friend laugh and say, "Yeah, that's it, that's funny."

Hugs, kisses, smiles, and squeals do not just happen anywhere. They only occur when the vibe is right, when the environment supports them. Like Natalia's classroom handshaking routine, they are forms of human care and recognition. They are things that help solidify the bonds that tie together families and communities, and their presence makes it easier to do the challenging work of social justice activism. In fact, Natalia's own stated philosophy about her teacher activism is instructive:

> In the end, what I'm trying to create in my classroom is an environment where my students feel empowered to do something different, think differently, love people, question, not just accept all the time. If that's what I'm trying to produce in my classroom, then they're gonna become social agents of change. Even if that means local, like in their families, if it means to challenge their mom, and their brothers and their sisters, I think that's a start. And it's through education that we can then prepare our children for the future and changing the course of history. I tell my students all the time, "You guys are history, you can create the future right now with the decisions you make, with the choices you make."

Whether she is in her classroom, home with her mother, at a NYCoRE meeting, or at a VB gathering, Natalia's focus is trained on building community and consciousness. For her, the relationships forged through working together, challenging each other, and learning from one another fuel her teacher activism. Changing the course of history means doing it together.

Part V: Reflections on Growing Consciousness and Community

Natalia's own consciousness was raised through a variety of experiences: family upbringing, childhood friendships, grade school, college, and student teaching. From each of these experiences, Natalia draws motivation or inspiration for her teacher activist work today. While her one classroom cannot replicate the vast array of political learning that Natalia has done throughout her life, she is intent on "planting seeds" and doing as much as she can to ensure that the learning experiences in her classroom move students forward on their own political journeys. In addition, as her teacher activism extends beyond the classroom, her activities focus on deepening others' political consciousness as well as continuing to develop her own. Her commitment to NYCoRE ItAGs is for the learning that they facilitate for teachers to improve their political practice. She recognizes the gaps in her own consciousness with respect to engaging in NYCoRE's union-related activism. Natalia also proactively expands her political consciousness by participating in VB. For Natalia, it is her consciousness that drives the change work in which she engages.

Freire (1993) articulated the power of critical consciousness. His educational theories posit that critical education—a praxis defined by a constant engagement in action and reflection—enables people to make sense of their own experiences and to challenge and change oppressive, unjust conditions. From her childhood inquiries about "Why are people so mean?" to her travel to Cuba to ensure that her own experience informs her assessment of the country's political history, Natalia's consciousness-building moments have resulted from reflection and action, and action and reflection.

However, essential to people's ability to engage in praxis is the extent to which they are supported to reflect and act. Thus, Natalia's focus on raising consciousness is also intimately tied to her emphasis on building community. For example, Natalia's classroom is carefully crafted: the classroom decorations, handshake routine, and curricular content are all elements that Natalia deliberately constructs. Most importantly, she works to build bonds of human connection and family-like ties that work to help students "feel empowered to do something different" and "become social agents of change."

Her focus on community building to support the development of political consciousness assigns greater weight to the significance of her original desires to become a teacher as a "helper" and "translator." Natalia shows how actions aimed at helping people feel more confident and comfortable are political acts to enable consciousness building. Opening a NYCoRE members meeting with a game of "Deejay" is not just for fun—it is to establish an environment that supports the reflection and action necessary for the political education that will follow. Her desire to create empowering space for NYCoRE members of color is directly tied to her sense that they need to feel supported and together to engage in NYCoRE's broader work.

Ultimately, Natalia's purpose of helping people to become agents of change, is rooted in community and consciousness. However, she is not prescriptive in the way that she expects students or teachers to go about making change in the future. She articulates a wide range of possibilities for change work: from challenging family members to changing the course of history. The emphasis in her statement to her students that "You guys are history, you can create the future right now with the decisions you make, with the choices you make" is on her students' power to make decisions and choices. Natalia's project as a teacher activist is not to steer people's actions in any particular direction, but more so to facilitate opportunities for them to grow consciousness and community by exploring their own lives, conditions, and experiences.

Note

1. On March 11, 2011, a devastating earthquake and tsunami struck Japan, killing thousands, and causing serious nuclear energy accidents, including meltdowns at numerous nuclear reactors.

References

Freire, P. (1993). *Pedagogy of the oppressed*. New York: Continuum.

KARI KOKKA: PLAYING THE GAME

Part I: The Rules

When Kari Kokka graduated with her master's degree and teaching certification from Stanford in 2001, her decision to move to New York City was impulsive. She found a cheap summer sublet apartment and only planned on checking out New York for a couple of months. Instead, Kari stayed through that first summer and found a job teaching math at Vanguard High School, a small, progressive school in Manhattan on the Upper East Side. Ten years later, this is the same school where I visit Kari's classroom for the first time.

Vanguard is housed within the Julia Richman Education Complex (JREC), which is also home to five additional autonomous schools. Including Vanguard, three of the schools located at JREC are members of the New York Performance Standards Consortium, a statewide consortium of 27 schools that oppose the use of high-stakes tests and have been granted waivers to employ performance-based assessments in lieu of New York State Regents Exams for high school graduation. I walk up the wide stone stairway to a set of large doors, which give way to a grand foyer of open space with vaulted ceilings and an expansive marble floor marked with columns that stretch out overhead. The security desk is set back toward the wall across from the entryway, almost an afterthought between two sets of swinging doors that lead into the auditorium. The two security guards glance over in my direction as I approach their desk. When I announce that I am here to visit Kari, they smile and nod and direct me to take the elevator to the fourth floor.

The open and inviting nature of this school building stands in stark contrast to the barracks-like security found in many other city public schools. In other schools, security stations are constructed as physical barriers immediately inside the entryway greeting visitors, students, and staff alike. Visitors must present identification, sign in on a visitor's log, and often proceed through a metal detector. In my experience, security officers at these schools can be gruff and unfriendly. School entryways, I find, say a lot about their prevailing cultural norms, expectations, and rules. The way I am greeted at Vanguard makes me feel welcomed as a first-time visitor.

I find Kari in the hallway before her 12th-grade math class is set to begin. She is dressed in her teaching garb—black pants with a light colored blouse covered by a black cardigan. Her straight black hair is slightly layered and falls below her shoulders and onto her back; her hair frames her face with a part on the left and is tucked behind her ears to keep it out of her eyes. We walk together to her classroom, marked by a brass plate bearing her name affixed to the wall next to the door. Inside, there are six rectangular tables, each with six chairs. She immediately busies herself prepping for class, writing the "Do Now" on the board at the front and the agenda on a poster hung to the right. The Do Now consists of two math problems:

1. Find the complex roots: $y = x^2 + 4x + 29$
2. Sketch a graph:
   a. w/ 2 single roots
   b. w/1 single root; 1 double root
   c. w/2 complex roots

Kari posts the quadratic formula underneath the first problem for reference. I ask her if there is anything I can do to help and she replies with a laugh, "Typical teacher mentality, always trying to do something."

Students arrive and quickly settle into their seats; they take out their notebooks and begin working on the Do Now. Clearly, the routine has been established and students know what to do without Kari's instruction. There are only 13 students in the class, six boys and seven girls, all Black or Latino. Vanguard draws most of its students from the predominantly Black and Latino neighborhoods of the Lower East Side (LES) and East Harlem. Kari continues to prepare for the day's lesson and the students work quietly. She finishes prepping and floats from table to table, checking on students' progress with the Do Now problems, offering help and answering questions.

At one point, she walks over to me with a book in hand. She puts it down in front of me on the table and says, "Isn't it interesting? This is what they're reading for English." The book, *Paper Son: One Man's Story*, is a memoir written by a Chinese immigrant who falsified documents identifying him as the son of a Chinese American to circumvent U.S. immigration laws, which put severe restrictions on any immigration from China between 1882 and 1943. "I have to tell you about a new Chinese American population in the ninth grade now," Kari adds as she walks away, back to her students. I remember a remark from one of our earlier conversations that Kari made when reflecting on her interest in issues of race and education, how she was a "Japanese American woman teaching in a school with not a single Japanese American kid, and maybe, like, one Asian American kid."

That there is a new Chinese American student population at Vanguard and that her English teacher colleagues introduced *Paper Son* to this year's curriculum are significant for Kari. Different from her experience in graduate school, where she felt Asian American students and perspectives were invisible to others, the introduction of *Paper Son* to the school curriculum underscores Vanguard's commitment to being a place where all feel invited to be part of the community, part of the conversation.

About 15 minutes into the class, Kari calls for volunteers to write their Do Now answers on the board. One student volunteers and Kari encourages another to go up for the second problem. While students are writing their answers on the board, she goes around to check on the others' work. "Oh, this is good," she says to some, and to others she asks questions about their work, such as "How did you get from this to this?" Students now become more animated, asking her for more help and chatting with one another.

After completing the Do Now, Kari sets up an activity called "Travelers and Tellers." Her demeanor is calm and her voice is soft and gentle; even as she reprimands students for cursing or chuckling at other students' answers, she is firm but nice. "Take out your packets," she says, and just as one student playfully sucks her teeth, Kari continues, "without sucking your teeth." She preempts the teeth sucking by knowing that it is coming. She knows her students and they know her; the young girl who sucks her teeth does it with a smile, teasing. The students all take out packets of math problems and arrange themselves at four tables, each representing a team. Kari asks each team to tackle two of the eight problems in the packet. She explains that teams will solve their assigned problems as a group and then draw up their solutions and explanations on poster paper. When they are finished, two tellers will stand at their posters, stationed to explain to others how they solved the problems. The remaining students will be travelers, moving from station to station in order to learn how each team arrived at its solutions. Then the travelers will rejoin their original group and teach the tellers about what they learned from everyone else.

The teams readily volunteer for problems and get to work on solving them together at their tables with impressive ease. The students seem comfortable and well practiced in working together. They are not only required to write down the answers to the math problems, but Kari also places an emphasis on students being able to verbally explain how they are thinking about and doing math. This emphasis means that students really talk and listen carefully to each other. It does not feel like many other classrooms that I have observed, where students talk only directly to the teacher, concerned with whether their answers are right or wrong.

Above the board at the front of the room hang reminders of the "Habits of Mind"—making connections, using evidence, considering viewpoints, being metacognitive, seeking significance, and asking "what if?"—and the "Habits of Work"—punctuality, organization, focus, cooperation, and revision—expected of all members of Vanguard classrooms. The 12th-graders in Kari's class have these habits well in hand, a result of three years of prior training as Vanguard students. The students are silly at times, laughing and joking with each other, but all are focused on getting their math problems solved.

Once teams hang their posters on the walls and assign tellers, the travelers move from station to station. I move between groups and listen in. The tellers are invariably confident and articulate with their answers. They explain their solutions step by step, and travelers do not hesitate to stop them and ask questions when details are not clear. As she observes student interactions, Kari tells students numerous times throughout the class to use "please" and "thank you." When students are presenting their work, she tells them to wait for the full attention of their classmates. She reminds students, "Please don't say shut up," and students apologize and ask their classmates to "please be quiet" instead. Students react to Kari's interventions with knowing assent; it is clear that these are not Kari's first times reminding them to be polite.

The class is running short on time before students are able to return to their original groups and reteach the solutions they have learned in their travels. Before closing out the activity, Kari makes sure to get everyone's attention and compliments the travelers and tellers, pointing out the good things she noticed during class. "David, the questions you were asking were right on point," she says. "And, Portia, you were very well prepared as a teller." When Kari compliments individual students, they say "thank you." The exchanges on the whole are respectful and genuine. She finishes by saying that they will complete the activity at the start of their next class and students are dismissed.

While I would not immediately characterize Kari's classroom as full of strict regimentation, there are plenty of expectations, both implicit and explicit, in her classroom pedagogy. There are expectations that students will take their learning seriously, that they will work together, and that they are confident in their ability to learn and do math. Explicitly, Kari reinforces the "Habits of Mind" and "Habits of Work" in her classroom. There is the expectation that students will talk to each other about their work and will do so politely. These expectations are emphasized in every teacher's classroom at Vanguard, but for Kari, they reinforce her belief that young people need to maintain a focus on academic rigor and learn how to behave in ways that will give them access to more opportunities in life. Kari's own life has taught her rules, both implicitly and explicitly, that have compelled her to become the teacher activist that she is today.

Kari grew up in San Jose, California, as a fourth-generation Japanese American. She jokes that she knows more of the Japanese language than her parents from a short time studying it in college. "Grandma can kind of speak," but as second-generation U.S.-born, even her Japanese language skills have faded. However, though Kari's family has been living on U.S. soil for more than a century, memories of the Japanese American internment during World War II (WWII) serve as reminders of how quickly U.S. society can turn on minority groups. Her mother was spared the experience of internment because she was not born until after the war, but Kari's maternal grandparents were sent to camps. Her father, with his parents and nine siblings, was interned. With this family history seared into her consciousness, Kari says that she "always had an interest in wanting to change things, or feeling like the system was not fair."

The legacy of the WWII internment for Japanese Americans is complicated. There were many who resisted and protested the camps. One widespread form of resistance was to answer "no" to two particular questions included in a questionnaire administered by the U.S. government upon internment. The questions, numbers 27 and 28, read as follows:

- Question #27: "Are you willing to serve in the armed forces of the United States on combat duty, wherever ordered?"
- Question #28: "Will you swear unqualified allegiances to the United States of America and faithfully defend the United States from any or all attack by foreign or domestic forces, and forswear any form of allegiance or obedience to the Japanese emperor, or other foreign government, power or organization?"

These questions were posed to U.S.-born Japanese Americans who, like Kari's family, had no ties to Japan and had lived in the United States for multiple generations. Insulted by the questions—first, because the government had the nerve to herd them into internment camps and then expect Japanese American men to serve in the military, and second because to "forswear any form of allegiance or obedience to the Japanese emperor" implied that there may have actually been an allegiance in the first place—many answered "no" to both as a form of protest. Dubbed "No-No boys," these protesters were sent to a particular internment camp in Tulelake, California, segregated as "disloyal" to the United States.

Kari was interested in hearing her relatives' opinions on details like the loyalty questions, but instead found her aunts and uncles unwilling to discuss such things. She tried to do a project in the seventh grade about her family's memory of the camps, but the memories seemed too painful for many of her family members to talk about. "I've definitely been yelled at for even asking questions," Kari reflects. "Like, 'Don't even ask me about that. You don't know how it was.'" One of Kari's uncles, who fought for the 442nd Regiment in the U.S. Army during WWII, hung up the phone on her when she called to interview him. Kari points out "the interesting thing is, even within the Japanese American community, that those who served in the 442nd are much more respected and revered than those who tried to stand up against the government, which is, I think, quite twisted."

The 442nd was a segregated all-Japanese American regiment and is still the most decorated unit in the history of the U.S. Armed Forces. Seen as redemptive war heroes who proved their loyalty and American-ness, men who fought as part of the 442nd were celebrated by the larger Japanese American community. Conversely, that same community distanced itself from resisters and protesters, leaving those like the No-No boys ostracized and marginalized by their own people. There were some relatives who talked to her, but they offered her "a really kind of one-sided view of like, 'Oh, we went to school, and this how it was, how the mess halls were where we ate.' But not so much like, 'Yeah, we felt like our rights were taken away from us.'"

The rules about justice, fairness, resistance, and protest conveyed by this history are confusing. On the one hand, the Japanese American internment has taught Kari that the rules of U.S. society are unfair. Fueled by her family history, Kari now has fierce reactions against racism and connects her work as a teacher activist to resisting the long-standing injustices facing people of color in the United States. On the other hand, resistance to the internment by the No-No boys was not rewarded, but the young men in the 442nd, who played by the rules, were cast as war heroes. The lesson taught by this bit of history seems to suggest that sometimes it is better not to openly resist injustice. Balancing between open protest and more subtle resistance is an act that Kari constantly negotiates as a teacher activist.

Kari's motivations to become a teacher stem from an underlying sense of unfairness that she developed from her schooling experiences. As a student at Independence High School in East Side San Jose, she "saw the disparities" in her honors classes where "there were a lot of White students," while they made up only ten percent of the student body. The majority of students, who were Vietnamese, Mexican, or Filipino, were underrepresented in honors classes. Kari says she "grew up feeling like it was completely unfair." However, it was not until Kari went to college at Stanford that she began to more fully grasp the injustices she grew up around. "I didn't know that Asian Americans make up four percent of the U.S. population," Kari says as she begins talking about her college experience. "Because everyone had black hair, everyone was the same height as me in high school, I was ignorant to the fact that I was in the minority. At Stanford, the first thing that I noticed was, 'Wow, in college everyone's really tall.'" Kari laughs as she recalls her reaction. "And, then I was like, 'Oohhhh, everyone's White.' And I think that's when I started to think a little bit more about looking at disparities and differences in opportunities."

Yet, Kari's commitments as a mechanical engineering major and member of Stanford's Division I diving team meant that she did not have time to be involved in much political work. Further, Kari says, "I was not politicized at all. There were definitely things going on you know, people were doing hunger strikes, and I was completely oblivious living in my little happy bubble." In fact, even though Kari starts her story of becoming a teacher with her reflections about racial disparities in her high school, her initial interest was more precipitated by deciding not to pursue a career in engineering. "I didn't really know what I was doing," she recalls. "I think it was my junior year that I decided that

I hated engineering, but I had to finish out my degree. [...] I did look into some engineering jobs. My job interviews were disasters, and I mean some of the jobs in mechanical engineering are going to work for someone who makes missiles. And then I did some others. I interviewed with LA Unified, who of course offered me a job on the spot, with Long Beach Unified, and then with Berkeley High." Kari went to visit Berkeley High School and "really loved the school." She accepted a job as a math teacher as part of an alternative certification program, but "it was kind of last minute, like 'Oh, let me be a teacher.'"

Kari describes Berkeley High School in ways similar to her own high school in San Jose. During her year at Berkeley, Pedro Noguera, then a professor at the University of California-Berkeley, published a paper exposing disparities between Black and White students at the school. The paper reported that while 60 percent of Black male students dropped out of Berkeley High, the school also sent more students to Harvard than any other public school in California. "The average grade point average for White students was a 3.1 versus a 1-point-something [for Black students]," Kari says. "And especially in math, you really saw the tracking." As a remedial prealgebra teacher, Kari taught a class that was all students of color, who, in her assessment, "shouldn't have been there. They should have been in a regular or an advanced class, but they had emotional or behavioral issues." A different teacher taught a calculus class in the same room and it was "mostly White students."

Noguera's research taught Kari language she could use to name her own accounts of an "unfair" system as products of institutional racism. As Kari came to understand how social factors produced the patterns of underrepresentation for students of color in honors and Advanced Placement (AP) classes, she began to see society in a new light. Her sense of unfairness identified as a youngster took new shape because she started to be able to analyze what it meant and where it came from. Now her math classroom takes shape as a place where she and her students can disrupt patterns of unfairness, rewrite the expectations that normally govern math class, and prepare to challenge the broader rules in society.

Part II: Understanding the Field of Play

Kari's hero is Yuri Kochiyama, one of the most prolific, if little celebrated, U.S. social justice activists of the 20th century. "I used to have this dream of wanting to open my own school," Kari says. "It would be called the Yuri Kochiyama

School for Social Justice." Kari continues, "I guess part of the reason why I admire her is because she was interned as my family was and because of all the work that she's done throughout her life and she's never given up, however old she is and still kicking."[1] Kochiyama was 20 years old when she and her family were sent to a Japanese American internment camp in Arkansas. Her first-hand experience of U.S. racial injustice sparked a lifetime of social and political activism. She was a well-known figure within the Civil Rights and Black Power movements with close ties to Malcolm X and joined a group of Young Lords who occupied the Statue of Liberty in 1977 to demand the release of Puerto Rican Nationalists from the U.S. prison system. A leader in the fight for reparations for Japanese American families who were interned, Kochiyama maintained involvement in social justice struggles, working to free U.S. political prisoners like Mumia Abu-Jamal and speaking out against U.S. imperialism.

Like Kochiyama, Kari's political activism did not begin until after graduating from college. Her first memory of feeling like a direct target of racism occurred shortly after she graduated from Stanford. She was leaving a nightclub in San Francisco with a friend and overheard a bouncer refer to her as "Oriental." She got upset and tried to "explain to him, 'We use that word for objects, not for people; it's considered a derogatory term.'" The bouncer's response was "nasty," which prompted Kari to start circulating emails within the Asian American community calling for a boycott of the club. Her emails drew the attention of the club's owner, who requested a meeting with Kari in order to apologize and get her to stop the call for a boycott. "Especially in San Francisco," Kari explains, "the Asian American population is big, so it's gonna make an impact if people decide to boycott." Kari's antiracist lens continued to sharpen after the incident at the nightclub.

Meanwhile, Kari struggled as a new teacher at Berkeley High and she did not feel that her alternative certification program was supportive. "It was absolutely horrible," Kari says. "I was learning literally nothing. So I quit the program, and then I went back to Stanford to do my master's and my certification." This time around, Kari entered Stanford with a focused political purpose. She credits the incident at the nightclub as having "solidified more why I wanted to become a teacher and opened my eyes more to how people are really ignorant." Particularly, as an Asian American, Kari developed a critical consciousness around the Model Minority Myth—the idea that Asian Americans, due to high levels of educational attainment and higher-than-average household incomes, serve as an exemplar for other racial minority groups in the United States. Long seen by Asian American activists as a divisive, overly simplistic, and inaccurate portrayal of Asian Americans, Kari spent significant energy pushing back against manifestations of the Model Minority Myth in her graduate school program.

"I was extremely vocal," Kari recalls. "To the point that I was probably not the most tactful person. My friend, he told me, 'You know what. People don't really comment in class anymore because they know you're going to jump down their throat.'" I smile when Kari tells me this, because I have also been known to jump into attack mode, perhaps too frequently, or at least prematurely. But listening to Kari tell it, every moment of her graduate program experience was laced with racist undertones. For her coursework, Kari's professors did not assign any readings about Asian American youth. Everything related to youth of color was about Black and Latino students, which Kari would have been willing to excuse if she was "someplace where there's not a large Asian American population." But Stanford is in the San Francisco Bay Area, where "the Asian American population is huge and people are still under the misconception of the model minority."

Kari sought to educate her peers about the challenges facing Asian American communities in the Bay Area. She organized a film screening, showing a documentary about Southeast Asian youth in the Tenderloin neighborhood of San Francisco. She shared information about the Mien community in Oakland, refugees from Vietnam. Her activities challenged her professors' lack of inclusion of Asian American perspectives in their curriculum and combated what she saw as the ignorance of many of her graduate student peers. "Some of the professors were not very receptive," Kari recalls in a frustrated tone. And she remembers typical comments coming from other graduate students who were student teaching in schools with Asian American populations, such as, "Because of the high Asian population, it's a very competitive school." The agitation is obvious on Kari's face when she rolls her eyes and exclaims, "Where did that come from!? What are you talking about!?"

The politicized Kari, the sometimes excitable and even angry Kari, is the person whom I get to know as a teacher activist. Rooted in a struggle against racism, she ties together her family's historical experiences of racial injustice with the everyday racism that she saw reflected in her own schooling experiences from San Jose to Berkeley to Stanford. For Kari, these formative experiences shape the field of play for her teacher activism; they are both the backdrop to her work and the roots from which she draws her motivation.

After graduate school, the transition from West to East Coast as an Asian American was challenging for Kari. She was living in LES, a neighborhood with a rich immigrant history that has undergone heavy gentrification with increased housing costs and more young, affluent White residents in the past 15–20 years. She remembers racial tension in her neighborhood. Being close to Chinatown meant that there were also significant numbers of Chinese residents in LES. Kari was particularly sensitive to the interactions she would observe between different people of color—Black, Latino, and Asian. "I did have some specifically anti-Asian incidents," she says. "And I'm always much more upset if it happens to me from another person of color than if it happens to me from a White person. But it also makes more sense to happen from another person of color because no one wants to be at the bottom of the totem pole. So I've really struggled with that, like why would this person, why would they do that to me if they know how it feels?"

In early 2005, Hot97, a local hip-hop radio station, played the "Tsunami Song" in the aftermath of the devastating Indian Ocean tsunami that claimed the lives of thousands of people in South and Southeast Asia. Hot97's "Tsunami Song" was an ill-advised and racist attempt at humor and included outrageously offensive and insensitive lyrics poking fun at the tragic loss of human life resulting from the disaster, referring to "screaming Chinks," "Africans drowning," "Little Chinamen" being swept away, and children being sold into slavery (Gothamist, 2005).

In response to the song's airing on the Hot97 morning show, Kari joined a coalition of hip-hop activists and Asian American organizations to form REACH—Representing Education, Activism, and Community through Hip-Hop. The group organized rallies to protest Hot97, demanding an apology and disciplinary action against the morning show personalities. They also conducted educational workshops and held events aimed at deepening people's understanding of hip-hop's history and positive potential. REACH included well-known activists like Rosa Clemente, who would run as the Green Party Vice Presidential candidate in the 2008 U.S. Presidential election, and DJ KuttinKandi, a Queens-native Filipina who was the first female turntablist to make it to the finals in the prestigious DMC USA deejay championships. Kari's relationships with the REACH community helped her establish better footing, connections, and confidence in New York City.

Because Hot97 is one of the most popular radio stations in the city, many of her students were aware of the "Tsunami Song" controversy. Kari told her students about the activist work that REACH was doing and one of her students, Jessica, wanted to get involved. Jessica went with Kari to a REACH protest and she spoke alongside local politicians and hip-hop artists. "She was the most captivating one of all," Kari smiles. "And she had never spoken up. She hated math class, she seemed completely disinterested in school. I had no idea how amazing of a young woman she was until we had talked about this issue together and she came and blew everybody away."

Kari began to get more involved in other activist work outside of school. She joined NYCoRE ItAGs, focusing on resisting military recruitment in schools and using media to teach for social justice. She would also make a point to tell her students about these activities and invite those who expressed interest. The leadership that students exercised as activists exposed Kari to a side of them that she had not seen in the math classroom. "The ones up at the mic speaking were always kids who I would've never have thought," Kari explains. "Kids who I had never heard articulate things that well [in class] would have this audience completely captivated. [...] They're so much more powerful as speakers. And they're the ones who need to be heard; they're the ones who create change. I just think that they have so much more potential than I do." Kari's activist work outside of school helped her rethink her relationships with students inside of school.

Like many small high schools, Vanguard has an "advisory" structure where each teacher is assigned to be the advisor for a small group of students with whom they meet regularly to build relationships and provide social, emotional, and academic support. The small-schools movement popularized advisory classes as a way to ensure that every student in a school is known well by at least one adult. When done well, advisory classes embody a school's commitment to close-knit and familial cultures. Although she was a skeptic of advisory when she first started teaching, now Kari reflects, "I think the advisory piece is really huge. I mean, my advisees are like my children. They'll call my cell phone, sometimes they'll text me like, 'Hey Mom, I'm not going to be in school tomorrow because I'm sick and I'm really sorry.' So that aspect I think is the best, this is home, I feel like it's family." Advisory classes at Vanguard are mixed by grade level, and whenever possible, students remain with the same advisor for their entire high school career.

I attend Kari's advisory class during one of my visits. Kari is sitting in a circle with her advisees and she motions for me to come join them. They are discussing how to handle different scenarios that teenagers commonly face in relationships and social situations. One student reads a scenario that describes a situation in which a girl is being pressured in her relationship to have sex with her partner. There is another scenario describing a student being bullied. Kari facilitates discussion about what students would do as individuals caught up in or observing these situations. These sessions help Kari get to know her students better by building their relationships outside of math class. She gets to talk to and advise students about the issues they face beyond math problems.

The advisory ends on a somber note, when a student reads an announcement about an upcoming memorial service for a former Vanguard classmate. Afterward, Kari explains that a former student, who would have been a senior this year, was shot and killed last week. There were grief counselors in school because a lot of the current seniors knew the student well. Many of the students who knew him are wearing RIP placards around their necks with a laminated picture of the young man and words commemorating his life. I see the same RIP posted in classrooms. In just a 20-minute observation, the importance of advisory in attending to the social and emotional needs of Vanguard students strikes home. Young people are engaged in struggles stemming from street violence to peer pressure on a daily basis. While they ostensibly come to school for academics, advisory class opens up the space for teachers and students to connect on a personal level, providing a circle of support though which students can face the additional struggles in their lives. This enables students to enter into the academic classroom more ready to learn.

While it took some time and adjustment for Kari to feel comfortable stepping into an activist role outside of her classroom in New York, she knew from the beginning that Vanguard offered her the playing field she needed for her activism inside the classroom. "I want to teach at a Title I school. I want to teach students of color. I want to teach kids who are behind in grade level," Kari proclaims. "Because those are the kids who need it the most and who've gone to schools where it's been completely unfair. They're not behind because they don't have the ability—they're just behind because they didn't have good math instruction from their K-8 school experience." At Vanguard, 80 percent of the students enter with math skills well below a ninth-grade level. Yet, "the work that we do with [students] by the time they're seniors, I think is amazing," Kari asserts. She is proud of the progress that the math department has made since she arrived at Vanguard. When Kari first started teaching at Vanguard, seniors were graduating based on their mastery of parabolas and linear functions. "They were doing ninth- and tenth-grade level work," Kari says, shaking her head. "And now we have AP Calculus, which was a pipe dream back then. That, I think, has been really inspirational."

Kari's classroom activism seeks to undo the unfairness meted out by her students' past educational experiences. And, for her, working with students to access math and build mathematical skills is its own social justice endeavor.

"Math is the gatekeeper through a lot of their standardized testing," Kari explains. For example, a score of 75 on the New York State Math Regents Exam exempts students from needing to pass the City University of New York's math entrance exam, meaning that they will avoid placement in non-credit-bearing remedial math courses in college. Kari believes that the work she and her colleagues do at Vanguard helps students "who maybe at another school would've completely fallen through the cracks."

Part III: Pedagogy of a Capoeirista

In graduate school, Kari's favorite book was Lisa Delpit's *Other People's Children*. Delpit (1995) calls for teachers to teach the norms and codes of privilege to help low-income students and students of color navigate systems that are governed by a dominant "culture of power." At the same time, teachers should work with students to resist these systems by instilling a sense of pride in their own cultural practices and modes of learning. For students like Kari's, calculus is often framed as something they cannot access because it is beyond their reach. Calculus is a subject reserved for the privileged few students who are "good" at math, who also often happen to ascribe to the dominant culture (i.e., they are White or affluent). Kari describes how dominant assumptions about teaching math feed into the patterns of disparity that prevent students who have historically struggled with the subject from taking calculus:

> People think of math and language as the linear subjects where you have to learn this thing and then one thing builds on top of the other. I will say the numeracy part can bog kids down and hinder their conceptual understanding. But their conceptual understanding isn't based just on their numeracy skills. So before I taught calculus, it was always taught where they did this algebra boot camp. The first month was all about catching kids up, like getting their fractions better, decimals, a lot of algebra skills better. I decided not to do that because I feel like if it's something that the kids already struggled with, why am I gonna remind them of the fact, like, oh, this is something that we all know that you're not good at so I'm gonna make you do it over again.

Instead, Kari's approach has been to teach students calculus concepts while supporting them to handle the more basic skills when necessary to solve calculus problems. "I mean my calculus kids still can't do fractions," Kari says, "but that doesn't mean they can't do calculus, right?" In other words, she provides access to a powerful form of cultural capital—calculus class—to students who would be traditionally excluded. She does not do this by harping upon or first insisting on "catching kids up" from their struggles with math in the past, but instead Kari engages students in learning calculus concepts and brushes up on their more basic skills "in a parallel fashion." And it seems to be working. In fact, about her current students, Kari says, "Their calculus is getting really good. They can tackle much more difficult problems without getting frustrated. My calculus kids right now, I would say, know more than the math teachers in my school."

Traces of Delpit's influence are evident in Kari's approach to teaching math. For Kari, teaching calculus to students who still struggle with more basic math challenges the dominant notion that many of her students are "bad at" or "don't get" math and gives students access to an important piece of cultural capital. Further, she disrupts the patterns of White dominance that she witnessed in higher-level math classes as a high school student and as a teacher in training. Whereas many young people are never afforded the opportunity to learn calculus, Kari's work changes the rules to the traditional math game and creates a new kind of calculus class open to all regardless of perceived skill level, disability, strengths, and weaknesses.

Yet Delpit's philosophy is not the only influence I find reflected in Kari's approach to teaching math. Kari first mentions her "Capoeira obsession" when she is lamenting her recent lack of active involvement with activist groups. "My Capoeira addiction is incurable," she says. "I used to go to lectures and panel discussions and book talks and NYCoRE stuff and now all I do is go to Capoeira class, like I'm crazy. […] I feel kind of guilty that my life has become just about me training Capoeira and not me helping anyone else or doing other things that I feel like I should be doing." Kari tries to "train Capoeira" on a daily basis, and while she says that it has taken her away from activist work, the more I learn from her, the more I start to think that Capoeira is actually operating at a deeper level, as a metaphor for her activist work. The rules, expectations, practices, and culture of Capoeira reflect and clarify Kari's activist values.

Capoeira's history is rooted in struggle. As early as the 17th century, it developed as a survivalist tool of self-defense for enslaved Africans brought to Brazil by Portuguese colonists. By the 19th century, it evolved as a tool for militarized resistance in the context of slavery in Brazil. Capoeira posed such a threat to Portuguese colonial rulers that its practice became severely restricted and those caught training faced harsh punishment. After the end of slavery in the late 19th century, the postcolonial Brazilian government continued to repress Capoeira and officially outlawed it in 1890. People continued to train in hidden or remote places and the martial art survived until the prohibition was lifted in

1940. Since the 1940s, Capoeira has flourished as a cultural practice. Its history has become a symbol of Afro-Brazilians' resistance to slavery and oppression and now people of all backgrounds in Brazil and around the world train Capoeira. In practicing Capoeira, Kari taps into its history of struggle and invokes the memories of her own family's oppression in Japanese American internment camps.

It is a Thursday evening in late September when I walk into the P.S. 321 gymnasium in Park Slope, Brooklyn—the venue for the week's New York Batizado. A batizado, which literally means baptism, is held to cultivate people's growth in Capoeira. The space is filled mostly by the capoeiristas who will be participating, about 50 in total. They are spread out across the gym, stretching, doing small jumping and kicking exercises, and getting ready for a night of competition. Kari arrives just as music starts to play and there is a callout in Portuguese. She says they are being called to start the evening with the opening "play." Kari warns me that once play begins, she will forget that there is anything else, that I am here, or even that she has work tomorrow. "I just get into a zone," she calls out as she jogs over to where the capoeiristas are forming a roda in the middle of the room.

One of the ways Capoeira survived through slavery was its subversive disguise. When training Capoeira, everyone stands or sits in a circle, called the roda, and there is a three-clap beat established along with singing and the playing of traditional Afro-Brazilian instruments. Slaveholders saw the music and accompanying martial arts moves as some sort of ritualistic dance, not as training for potential combat, and enslaved Africans would often practice in plain sight.

At the batizado, the opening play functions as a warmup for everyone—the musicians and the participants. In the roda, one main singer uses a microphone, leading a song, but everyone else is expected to sing in response while clapping and lending their energy. Players take turns, two at a time, entering the middle of the roda. When another person steps into the middle, the player who has been there the longest rotates out. There does not seem to be any particular order to who goes in when, and some players go into the middle multiple times, while others do not go at all. People are clearly at all different skill levels as some are faster, slower, more or less graceful, and more or less acrobatic in their movements. Men and women do play together, although it often seems that the pairs ebb back and forth between single-sex duos. When two capoeiristas enter into the middle of a roda, their play represents the artful combat training that was key to Capoeira's strategy of subversive resistance. For their moment in the roda, the two act as opponents, but they also engage figuratively in conversation. Their training helps them think about strategies for victory, each carefully observing the other to figure out when best to deploy offense versus defense, seeing and seizing opportunities to move from lying low to displaying a powerful jump, kick, swipe, or spin. Historically, these were skills enslaved Africans practiced in case they were needed for self-defense or open rebellion.

Kari jumps into the opening play two different times and I notice that her movements are a bit faster and smoother than a lot of the other players. Though she is relatively short, standing tall at just inches above five feet, Kari's kicks can clear impressive heights when she is on the offensive. Her athletic body moves with the fluidity one might expect from a former gymnast and collegiate diver. However, one reason Kari is drawn to Capoeira is its open acceptance of anyone who would like to join the roda, regardless of athletic prowess. "There's a guy that we train with," Kari says. "He doesn't have legs so he has these things that only go up to his knee but he plays Capoeira. And even in Brazil they teach to children with severe special needs. I've even seen kids in wheelchairs and someone will push them around."

Kari explains that you cannot do Capoeira by yourself because you need a circle; you need people to play instruments, clap, and sing. Without these elements, Capoeira is incomplete. "I don't like to sing, but you need to sing," Kari shares. "You learn all the instruments so some people are really good. They have a really great voice; they're really good on a certain instrument. The physical part of it some may not be as strong at, but everyone has something to contribute regardless." Together, the Capoeira family supports its members to improve upon their strengths and take risks trying something new.

Kari's description of her Capoeira community sounds a lot like her description of Vanguard and her math pedagogy. Her training at Stanford focused on a teaching methodology called "complex instruction," which stresses group work, mixed ability classrooms, and performance-based assessment. "One thing that's really big to me is having kids help each other," Kari explains. "And not only because just, in general, I want my kids to grow up to be helpful, respectful people but also there's been research to show that in math working in groups is actually more effective for kids than lectures. So facilitating a lot of group work is good teaching in math." The careful organization of her classroom seeks to ensure that there is space and opportunity for students to work together. From volunteering students to share their Do Now solutions to teaming up as travelers and tellers, students in Kari's math class are all part of an ongoing dialogue about math.

If her own classroom functions as a kind of math roda, welcoming as many students as possible to gain access to the powerful practice of math, then her work outside the classroom is focused on widening the circle of math educators who might teach with similar purpose. In 2007, Kari was a participant in a NYCoRE ItAG examining ways to counter military recruitment of students in NYC public high schools. She and another participant, Jonathan Osler, who was also a math teacher, started to have side conversations about social justice math teaching. One day, Jonathan asked Kari, "Would you be down to organize a conference with me?" Without really knowing what Jonathan had in mind, Kari said, "Yeah, sure." Kari chuckles at the memory, "We were talking about it and who could be a keynote speaker and he said, 'I really want to get Bob Moses.' So then at that point the light bulb goes off in my head, I'm like, 'OK, you're thinking big nationwide conference!'"

Bob Moses' life as an activist and career as a math educator is long and storied. In his early 20s, he was one of the leaders of the Student Nonviolent Coordinating Committee (SNCC), which coordinated some of the most successful activism in the Civil Rights Movement—especially with respect to voter registration drives in the South. Years after the Civil Rights Movement, Moses had children in the Cambridge Public Schools in Massachusetts and was dismayed by the education they were receiving. In response, he started the Algebra Project. At first a school-based curriculum program to improve math instruction in Cambridge, the Algebra Project has since grown into a national organization promoting rigorous math instruction and social justice activism through its sister organization, the Young People's Project.

Kari knew that securing Dr. Moses as the keynote speaker for the conference would lend a high level of credibility to their effort, and to their seriousness about both math and social justice. Sure enough, the first conference, which they would call Creating Balance in an Unjust World, attracted more than 500 participants from 28 states, Canada, and even Australia. "I mean it was just really great because there was really no other conference like it," says Kari. "Not one so specific to math and social justice."

The conference continues to attract participants from across the country and remains one of a kind. I attend the third Creating Balance conference in October 2010 at Long Island University's downtown Brooklyn campus. I meet Kari, who is armed with a walkie-talkie to communicate with other conference organizers. She is shuttling back and forth between the registration table, auditorium, and workshop classrooms to ensure that everything is ready before the opening keynote address. She is nervous because she has to introduce this year's keynote speaker and has not met her before.

Dr. Joi Spencer, assistant professor in the School of Leadership and Education Sciences at the University of San Diego, arrives and Kari greets her with a warm hug and smile. They talk with each other and move to the front of the auditorium to set up the PowerPoint and conduct a sound check for Dr. Spencer's talk. Conference participants begin streaming into the auditorium to claim seats and when the clock strikes nine, there are at least 100 people present for the Saturday morning start. The crowd is diverse, comprising young and old, Black, White, Latino, and Asian, current classroom teachers, aspiring teachers, and university-based math educators.

Dr. Spencer's talk, "Take a stand to keep your seat in the classroom," centers on the relationships between math instruction and racial disparities in educational outcomes. She traces the "disintegration and downfall" of the African American community in LA that coincided with the rise of crack cocaine spreading on the streets. She stresses that the social context and history of cities and communities matter, and that teachers' personal connections to their work are important. What teachers bring to their work as individuals—their personal backgrounds and experiences—shape their approaches to and passions for teaching. Dr. Spencer talks about teacher dispositions toward students and declares that "if your ideas about the kids you're teaching don't change, we could do lesson study forever and it won't matter." I notice Kari nodding in agreement and think about how much emphasis she has placed upon building strong relationships with her students. After the keynote is over, the audience, which has ballooned to more than 200 people, is excited. They give Dr. Spencer an energetic ovation and Kari surveys the crowd with a beaming smile on her face. The keynote has struck the right balance, one that I have seen in Kari's practice, between stressing the importance of rigorous math learning for all students and fighting back against an inequitable system that oppresses low-income communities and communities of color.

Creating Balance has developed into a space for math teachers to explore and improve their practice as social justice educators. For organizers like Kari, the conference is a tool for disrupting the injustice of "the system" that they deeply distrust. Yet, interestingly, the conference has also received mainstream support. Mirroring Capoeira's origins of training for resistance in plain sight, and much to the chagrin of conservative education commentators in New York City (Stern, 2007a; 2007b), the Department of Education (DOE) has been a conference sponsor and supporter. In addition, Math for America, which Kari views as "an extremely conservative organization," was a sponsor for the first Creating Balance conference. The commitment to rigorous math education, a value held by both mainstream education reformers and more radical educators, has enabled Creating Balance to carve out activist space with the support of the very system it seeks to challenge.

Kari's Capoeira teacher emphasizes that the martial art is a creative blend of "playfulness, history, tradition, respect, attack, defense, and conversation." These elements are the values of a capoeirista, but they are also what Kari integrates into her math pedagogy. Evidenced in her classroom practice and at the conference, she is motivated by an understanding of the historical oppression of communities of color. Kari builds expectations of respect and playfulness into her teaching, but she also never loses sight of her belief that math is a weapon to be forged for attack and defense against an unfair system.

Part IV: Earning Cords

At the batizado event, the capoeiristas are all dressed in matching uniforms: T-shirts emblazoned with the New York Batizado logo and white sweat pants with belt loops holding different colored rope cords. "You start out with a raw cord, and then you get half raw/half yellow, then full yellow, and then it goes in half steps," Kari explains. "So after yellow is orange, then blue, green, purple, brown, red." Kari's hard training has seen her progress steadily from her initial raw cord to a full orange cord. After the batizado, Kari will earn an orange/blue cord, one step below full blue. "In Capoeira, it all just depends on what your teacher thinks, and [the batizado] is only once a year," she says. "So if you're not really training, you're not going to get a new cord." Given this explanation, it is clear that training Capoeira is a serious commitment, one that takes focus and time. Mastery is not something that is achieved easily and one's accomplishments honor and respect the legacy of those who have come before.

Back at Vanguard, Kari works hard to help students demonstrate their mastery of math. This mastery is on display during students' Performance-Based Assessments (PBAs), done at the end of each school semester. PBAs are serious business at Vanguard, as they are graduation requirements. Students must choose between their 11th- or 12th-grade classes for their math PBA. This year, Kari has five students in her AP Calculus class who need to fulfill their graduation requirement with an AP Calculus PBA. For students, their PBAs represent the ultimate demonstration of their math learning. It is where they finally put on display for others to see what they have learned and how deeply they understand it.

When I visit Kari's classroom in early June, it is time for students to complete their PBAs. I find Kari talking to some students by her desk. There are small groups of students working at the computers, editing their PBA Power-Point presentations and practicing with partners. The first thing Kari says to me is, "I'm stressed." I know from recent email exchanges that she is very busy and stressed out over the PBAs for her 12th-graders. She is exhausted from 12-hour days at school and missing Capoeira training. The atmosphere in the room conveys what compels Kari to stay hours after school to work with students on their final PBA preparations. While not a traditional exam, the PBAs are still high stakes and students understand the serious pressure behind their successful performances. Kari seems to take on her students' stress and worries herself as she becomes obsessed with students being prepared, doing well, and passing.

Kari is visibly nervous, pacing back and forth between different students, asking them about their last-minute preparations and offering them food to eat, fulfilling her "motherly" duties as their teacher and advisor. Spring PBAs are most stressful since for 12th-graders, the outcome will determine their eligibility for graduation in just a few weeks. As a visitor, Kari asks me to serve as an informal observer for some of the PBAs and sends me off to a classroom. I find the room and meet Carina, who will be presenting her AP Calculus PBA. Her audience includes two teachers (one math and one humanities), an 11th-grade student, her math student mentor (a fellow AP Calculus student who already passed her math PBA in 11th grade), her mother, and me. Carina is dressed up for the occasion, wearing a black skirt suit with pumps and a tank top blouse with decorative sequins.

The PBA is designed to have students "teach" calculus to their audience, moving from basic foundational concepts to more advanced ones. The PBA culminates by requiring students to teach the solution to a complex problem that is taken from the open response section of a practice AP exam. Carina reviews limits, followed by derivatives, integrals, and antiderivatives. Her review connects these concepts to problems of calculating velocity and acceleration. Right away, her high level of preparation is evident as she is able to walk through detailed PowerPoint slides displaying the concepts and problems without any notes. She speaks confidently and smoothly, and fields questions and inquiries from her audience without missing a beat. As I have seen in Kari's classes, Carina's performance is an example of the ease with which Vanguard students talk about their work, answer challenging questions, and are willing to stand in front of an audience to demonstrate what they know.

At the end of her presentation, Carina goes to wait in the hallway while the PBA committee deliberates. There is no question in anyone's mind that she has passed and they discuss both positive and constructive feedback to give to her when she returns. After her committee calls her back into the room to inform Carina that she has passed, we both return to Kari's classroom to share the good news. Kari and another teacher are there with a handful of students who are making their last-minute PBA preparations. Carina's announcement that she has passed is greeted with a round of applause and Kari squeals with delight as she gives Carina a warm embrace. For Kari, the embrace is not just to congratulate Carina—it also serves as a cathartic release of emotion built up over the course of teaching her AP Calculus class.

In years past, when Kari was not the calculus teacher, many students who had already met their math graduation requirements (seven semesters of math credits and a math PBA) dropped AP Calculus in the spring. This year, Kari told her students that this was not acceptable. In addition, she did not allow students who needed to pass their math PBA to give their presentations in the fall so that they would stay committed and engaged through to the spring. Students who had done their math PBA in 11th grade were assigned as "mentors" for their peers who still needed to pass the math PBA. As mentors, students helped their partners prepare, practice, and perfect their PBAs. There were three students who were not assigned as mentors, and they were instead required to do an in-class presentation, which served as a model PBA for those who were preparing their official ones. This class structure for the second semester focused everyone on continued learning and growth, whether it was their own or their partners'. She also made sure everyone in class took the AP Calculus exam, something that had not happened in the past.

These hard-nosed decisions reflect one final aspect of Kari's teacher activist approach. As if taking cues from Capoeira's rigorous training and process of earning cords, Kari ensures that her students work and train hard to earn their academic accolades. She does not allow for shortcuts and holds all of her students to high expectations. She sees her approach as ensuring that her students gain access to opportunities and are able to "play the game."

"You know, even though I hate the system, I'm going to play the game to get what I want to get for myself or for my kids," Kari says. "Which is not the same outlook that other teacher activists have. I think that some people are against even having to play the game at all." For Kari, "the game" she talks about is a metaphor for navigating the complex social, political, and economic systems set up to the advantage of some players and the disadvantage of others. Having learned the rules of the game and being trained how to play, she believes in her ability to navigate these structures. As a teacher activist, she wants to support and guide her students to play the game to the best of their abilities. She sees the option of not engaging in the game as unproductive, hence her not allowing students to opt out of calculus class or the AP exam.

Using an example of educators who advocate for doing away with the practice of grading, Kari says, "It's OK for people who are empowered already to say 'I'm not going to play by the rules' versus if I'm not empowered and then I'm also not going to play by the rules. So I'm going to take away grades—now what are they going to look at? They're going to look at my SAT score, which isn't as great as my grades and then I have no grades to boost me up. So I don't like putting my kids in jeopardy where I feel like other people are more privileged to do that because they're coming from a different place." Kari's approach to her activist work, then, is calculated with respect to how she is positioning herself and her students to become empowered by gaining access to the game. "They," in her statements like these, are those people with power and privilege—the gatekeepers and decision-makers who often use the rules to favor others like them and disadvantage students like Kari's who come "from a different place." Her effort is to ensure that her students can stand on accomplishments that translate into the currency of the system, even if she hates that system and deems it unfair.

As a teacher activist committed to "playing the game" in ways that benefit those who the rules are set up to disadvantage, returning to Capoeira as a metaphor offers a whole new set of rules. Like a roda, her classroom pedagogy is intent on inclusion and collaboration. The literal conversations that her students have about math learning parallel the figurative conversations capoeiristas conduct through their movements. The surface of her teaching activism, whether in her classroom or at Creating Balance, dons the rhetorical cloak of mainstream math rigor, while simultaneously aiming to train and prepare young people and teachers to resist the system. The functionality of math knowledge for Kari is not about advancing careers in the science, technology, engineering, and mathematics (STEM) fields. Instead, math knowledge for Kari serves as an entrée into social justice work. She has forged math into a tool to help young people in schools like Vanguard to overcome the unfairness of the system and gain access to the system with the hopes of subverting it. Her Capoeira teacher says, "When inside and part of the roda, all speak the same language of Capoeira, and all feed off of the energy provided by the roda." Kari may teach math, but she speaks capoeira.

Part V: Reflections on Playing the Game

Kari cites Lisa Delpit's (1995) *Other People's Children* as an influential text for her graduate school learning. A compelling "both/and" argument, Delpit's work has influenced the practice of many educators who grapple with the dilemma of teaching students how to survive within an unjust system, but also thrive on their own terms and challenge and change the system. A different perspective is that of Lorde (1984), who famously warns that "the master's tools will never dismantle the master's house. They may allow us to temporarily beat him at his own game, but they will never enable us to bring about genuine change" (p. 112). If change is the objective in terms of the game, then it seems that energies should be focused on creating a new game, not learning how to play by the rules of the current one.

Kari firmly establishes her fundamental distrust for the system and also identifies injustices she personally observed throughout her own schooling experiences. However, Kari herself gained access to higher-level classes and attended an exclusive university in Stanford. In other words, she was given access to the game, taught the rules, and played it very well. Perhaps this personal history influences her sense of justice as a teacher focused on using math to help her students gain access to the game as well. She is explicit in her desire to play the game to the advantage of herself and her students. In fact, Kari introduces Lorde's quotation during one of our conversations, and follows it up by saying, "I don't know if I entirely believe that, maybe I have to be part of the system if I want to change it." Thus, as much as she distrusts and dislikes the system, she sees no choice other than to engage with it. Kari's reflection may also be interpreted as a statement of the tension that faces oppressed peoples, summarized by Ella Surrey, an elderly Black woman domestic worker, who asserts, "we know we have to play the game. We've always had to live two lives—one for them and one for ourselves" (Gwalteny in Collins, 2009, p. 107).

However, understanding Kari's philosophy and approach to teacher activism as merely playing the game is inadequate. First, her heroine, Yuri Kochiyama, can hardly be characterized as someone who played the game in her activist work. Kari's own rejection of the Model Minority Myth and her activism asserting a fuller picture of and respect for the experiences of oppression facing Asian Americans represent an overt challenge to the game. In addition, her personal commitment to the practice and lifestyle of Capoeira provides a lens that complicates any simple interpretation of her actions as teacher activist. In particular, Capoeira's history and philosophy force us to consider the subversive nature of what Kari is doing when she appears to play the game.

The game that Kari plays is complicated. To her, students are not just learning math. She is intent on helping her students gain skills that will provide access to opportunities to play society's games at large, but she is also simultaneously subverting the normative rules, which would prevent many of her students from having a chance to play in the first place. When it comes to calculus, she does not believe that the game is just for those people who happen to be "good at math," but instead that it is for everyone and that everyone can be good at math. The confidence of her students and their abilities to talk and inquire about math learning stems from Kari's pedagogy that reconstitutes the rules of the traditional math game so that it can be played by her students. These are the subtle tweaks Kari makes in order to play the game to get what she wants for herself and for her students. Kari's hope is that with the skills and access that her teacher activism facilitates, she and her students will play the game, change the face of the game, and eventually rewrite the rules.

Note

1. Yuri Kochiyama passed away on June 1, 2014 at the age of 93.

References

Collins, P.H. (2009). *Black feminist thought: Knowledge, consciousness, and the politics of empowerment*. New York: Routledge Classics.

Delpit, L. (1995). *Other people's children: Cultural conflict in the classroom*. New York: The New Press.

Gothamist. (2005). Hot97 is in hot water. Retrieved July 17, 2012, from http://gothamist.com/2005/01/24/hot_97_in_hot_water.php

Lorde, A. (1984). The master's tools will never dismantle the master's house. In A. Lorde, *Sister outsider: Essays and speeches by Audre Lorde* (pp. 110–113). Berkeley, CA: Crossing Press.

Stern, S. (2007a, March 19). Radical equations. *City Journal*. Retrieved September 15, 2013, from http://www.city-journal.org/html/eon2007-03-19ss.html

Stern, S. (2007b, May 11). Radical math at the DOE. *City Journal*. Retrieved September 15, 2013, from http://www.city-journal.org/html/eon2007-05-11ss.html

LISA NORTH: BUILDING SOLIDARITY

Part I: Being Seen and Seeing Others

Lisa North's memories of elementary school are sobering. Her elementary school was "a very typical rural Southern school," where students were expected to sit with their hands folded and told: "Be quiet and don't say a word." For her part, in the elementary grades, Lisa "hated school" and found it to be "really boring." She would "try to be sick" so that she could stay home and stay away from school, but her mother would only let that happen if she actually had a fever, something that Lisa found was hard to fake. Lisa frequently "got in trouble for talking" and often had to stay in for recess to write, "I must not talk, I must not talk, I must not talk," over and over again on a piece of paper.

One time in fourth grade, Lisa was punished for turning around and talking to students sitting behind her. When she was turned around, her teacher came by and said, "Well, if you like to face the back of the room so much, you can turn your whole desk around and face the back of the room." The teacher made Lisa turn her desk to face the back so that she actually had to twist in her seat to see what was happening at the front of the room. When Lisa arrived at school the next morning, she found that her friend who sat next to her had turned her desk around too. Together, they sat facing the back of the room. Lisa remembers sitting like this for about a week before the teacher, who would pace up and down the aisles while students were doing their work, suddenly stopped, as if seeing this pair of students facing the opposite direction for the first time. "So, you turned your desk around?" she asked Lisa's friend. "Yes, I did," replied the friend defiantly. And then the teacher just kept walking. Eventually, when parent-teacher conferences were approaching, Lisa was afraid that her mother would be upset if she saw her desk facing the back of the room. She asked her teacher, "Do you think I could turn my desk back around now?" The teacher gave permission and Lisa and her friend faced the front of the room again.

More than 50 years later, her friend's small act of solidarity has remained in Lisa's memory. Perhaps this is because in elementary school, Lisa felt that kids were treated like they did not exist, like "they were things." In the lunch-room, for instance, when students lined up to get their food, teachers would cut in front of the line whenever they pleased, without so much as a nod or any acknowledgement of the students they were stepping in front of. Lisa remem-bers feeling invisible when that would happen. At least in her fourth-grade classroom, Lisa knew that she was seen by her friend who acknowledged Lisa's presence by taking it upon herself to sit with Lisa facing the back of the room. When she got to middle school, Lisa noticed a stark difference. "I loved middle school," Lisa recalls. There, teachers who came to the front of the lunch line would say, "Excuse me, miss." For Lisa, this was "amazing" and she felt "vali-dated as a human being for the first time" by an adult in school.

Now, with more than 20 years of experience, Lisa has taught in two dif-ferent New York City (NYC) public elementary schools. Most recently, she was working as a literacy coach at PS 3, The Bedford Village School, but due to budget cuts eliminating many of the coach positions, she has transitioned back to the classroom and teaches second grade. The school and the neigh-boring city park and playground occupy a full square block in the heart of the Bedford-Stuyvesant neighborhood in Brooklyn. It is a predominantly African American neighborhood, with smaller and more recently immigrated African and South Asian Muslim families. This diversity is reflected in the student body of about 600 children and, if one listens carefully throughout the day, a local mosque's prayer calls can be heard throughout the neighborhood. The school's strong roots in the community are evident in the fact that some teachers and the principal are actually PS 3 graduates, but Lisa also mentions that it is the oldest continuous school in the city, having been established in the early 1700s. The main office bulletin board displays pictures of African American histori-cal figures along with short biographies—Mary Bethune, Maya Angelou, and

Martin Luther King Jr.—who serve as role models along with the school's principal and many of Lisa's teacher colleagues, who are African American.

In contrast to her own negative elementary school memories, Lisa wants to be a teacher who helps students "fall in love with" learning. Her "happiest" moments while teaching are when "the kids are engaged and they are interested in what they are doing." She believes that these moments most often occur when students are able to bring their own selves into and personally connect with their learning. Remembering a writing unit she did with students when "the kids were writing about their own experiences," Lisa reflects that students "enjoyed it because it was about something that they were invested in—their own story." Further, she also stresses how important elementary school is for the socialization of students, so that they understand how to live, work, and play together. Good teachers, according to Lisa, are able to understand what their students need and structure learning environments that support them. The challenge lies in the complexity of needs, which are on full display each time I visit her classroom.

Lisa's classroom is colorful. Immediately past the doorway is a primary color-blocked area rug just large enough for about 20 seven- and eight-year-olds to sit together. The perimeter of the room is lined with bookshelves and storage bins on one side and coat hooks and cubbyholes labeled with students' names on the other. The walls are adorned with large alphabet letters, a poster-size multiplication table, an oversized calendar with a birthday chart, a vocabulary word wall, and classroom rules. Student work hangs down from strings that crisscross overhead, completing the fully utilized, almost over-packed space. Desks are clustered into groups of four and there is a half moon-shaped table in the back where I find Lisa and her coteacher sitting together before the school day is about to begin. Lisa has thick dark brown hair, which is invariably pulled back into a ponytail, leaving short bangs that fall across her forehead. She stands tall at about five feet eight, and looks almost silly sitting in a child-size chair surrounded by piles of student worksheets and folders.

Lisa and her team teacher are making last-minute preparations and decisions for the day's lessons. They discuss when to do math, when to do reading, and how to squeeze in social studies. It turns out that five additional students have been added to their class for six weeks due to a teacher being out on maternity leave. Instead of hiring a long-term substitute, the school principal decided to break up the class and redistribute the students across the other three second-grade classrooms in order to save money. Now, instead of 16 students, Lisa's class has 21, a significant jump. Two of the students temporarily assigned to Lisa's class have behavioral challenges and are known to be "problems" throughout the school. Lisa admits that "it's tiring," with an exasperated sigh, almost searching for some sort of answer that I might provide to help alleviate the challenging situation, but instead all I can offer is an extra adult body for the morning.

When it is time, I follow Lisa and her team teacher down to the auditorium to pick up their students. No sooner than when we enter the auditorium, where students gather before being led as a group by their teachers to their classrooms, are we met with a wave of important student needs. Tristan is sick and not feeling well, Sheldon has a black eye that needs inquiring about, Usef is sitting by himself away from all the other students with his head bowed and downcast eyes—and all this with only 11 of the 21 students being present. Lisa quickly checks in with each of her students and then goes over to Usef, who is one of the five students temporarily placed in the class, to see why he is sitting alone and to coax him into joining the rest of the class to go upstairs.

Soon after we go back to the classroom, another seven students arrive, pushing the attendance up to 18, a more full class. The start-up of class feels haphazard as students get settled with so many streaming in late. The morning announcements begin on the intercom. Some students recite a daily affirmation: "My heritage is one of greatness and I know that I can do more. I must never, ever do less than those who came before," and then the principal makes some announcements. The principal begins to announce the science fair winners and Lisa calls for everyone's attention when the second-grade winners are to be revealed. Students quiet down and listen for the names of their classmates. When a student is named, classmates clap and seem genuinely excited. When the announcements end, everyone goes back to what they were doing previously.

From the start, it seems like it is going to be a challenging day. The students are rambunctious and testing their teachers' patience. They all want help with their academic work and they vie for attention by acting out demonstrably. Gabrielle waves her hands wildly, loudly proclaiming that she needs help. Tristan puts his head down on his desk, burrowing into his arms in an effort to both disappear and be noticed. Rebecca usually finishes her assignments without too much assistance, but then seeks teacher approval for each piece of her work.

And the needs go beyond academic work. Gian, who is otherwise a gentle, sensitive boy, is easily agitated and can lash out at students when his frustration boils over. If an adult can pull him aside to calm him down one-on-one, he is able to regain control over his emotions and anger. I happen to be the closest adult when he yells at his neighbors and pushes his chair over. I talk to him quietly and he calms down and asks, "Why am I this way?" I don't have an answer. All students need attention, care, and love from someone they can trust to help them with whatever it is that they are going through at the moment, from not understanding the math problem to trying to figure out why they have a hard time controlling emotions.

If a teacher's responsibility is to understand what her students need, then it is further complicated by the current education reform context of increased curricular rigidity and a narrowed focus on defining student success by standardized test outcomes. For example, basal readers—a series of books used to teach reading—are part of the mandated literacy curriculum for Lisa and her colleagues. "I really feel that for kids to become what they like to call 'lifelong readers,'" Lisa explains, "they have to fall in love with a series; they have to enjoy some book and then say, 'Oh, I am going to read the next one and the next one and the next one.'" She continues, "Unfortunately, basal readers don't do that." Lisa finds that "Basal readers are so concentrated on teaching comprehension strategies, they take away from the enjoyment of reading." She explains that if you only use basal readers, then students do not have a chance to fall in love with "actual reading," which includes students having the opportunity to immerse themselves in a story and talk with each other about how stories relate to life.

Due to these limitations and those of other mandated curricula, Lisa and her team teacher sometimes end up lacking passion for what they need to teach. When Lisa and her grade team meet, they do not have time to discuss individual students and their needs or innovative ways to plan curricula. "I mean, we do have a common planning period, but it's usually to talk about tests," Lisa laments. "What's the next test? What are we going to do about this test? We need to come up with a homework packet. It's not about curriculum. We don't talk about how we're going to plan curriculum at all." They are handed the curricula from which they are not supposed to deviate and told that they need "to move" their students "through" it. This movement, then, becomes their focal point and the barometer for success.

However, each time I visit Lisa's classroom, I watch as she tries her hardest to attend to the social and emotional needs of her students. If anything can characterize her students' behavior, it is their need to be seen, heard, and understood. She consistently sits down next to her students or pulls them aside and talks to them calmly and soothingly. She asks them questions about what might be bothering them or what it is that they need, after which she does the best she can to help them move forward with their academic work.

The lesson she learned as an elementary school student was that adults did not see or understand her, and this is not a lesson she wants to repeat.

If Lisa's elementary school experience made her feel invisible and unseen, her parents taught her how to recognize and see all members of their community. Lisa's rural southern school served the small farming town in southern Maryland "tobacco country" where she grew up. "My school bus driver was a tobacco farmer," Lisa says. "He kept the bus in the tobacco barn." The town was an hour south of Washington, D.C., or to be more specific, Lisa describes, "go to Mount Vernon in Virginia and if you look across the Potomac River you see the area where I grew up." When her parents moved there in the late 1940s, there was only one two-room schoolhouse. They worked hard with other community members to get a "regular elementary school built" that Lisa and her older sister would attend.

The town was "very racially segregated" and "the community was mostly White." Lisa, who is White, remembers her parents making efforts to work with Black community members. They "made it a point" to hire Black workers when they were building a new house and Black teenage girls to babysit Lisa and her sister. "So I grew up with Black people around [...] not so segregated," Lisa explains. "But if it was any social situation, like at school, it was pretty separate." It surprises me that a White family hiring Black people would stick out in Lisa's mind as some type of effort to integrate racially. I ask Lisa if even this level of interaction between White and Black people in her town was uncommon and her reply painfully illustrates the deep-seated racism surrounding her where she grew up:

> Well, I didn't even think about it until later when I got into middle school, and that's when I realized that these other people out there were very racist. My friends, they called me "nigger lover" and all kinds of things.

Because of her family's reputation for being friendly with the Black community, Lisa tells me, "When they integrated the school, they called my mother. The principal was worried there was going to be trouble, so she called and asked her to be there to greet the Black parents when they came in." With shades of Little Rock, Arkansas in 1957, where Black students needed armed National Guard escorts to safely enter a previously all-White school, Lisa describes what her mother told her about integration in their town in the mid to late 1950s.

When Mrs. North arrived at the school on the first morning of integration, she was stationed out by the front door. White parents began to gather around the school entrance, creating an intimidating barrier for Black families as they arrived with their children. When Black families arrived, Mrs. North moved out beyond the front of the crowd, striding confidently with her arms extended in greeting. "Hello, Mrs. Johnson! How are you? It's so nice to see you!" she exclaimed, welcoming families to the school. She then turned back toward the crowd and walked with each family to the main entrance. A friendly and familiar face, Mrs. North greeted Mrs. Johnson and more Black mothers, helping quell the tensions that literally surrounded the school on that first day of racial integration.

Lisa's sister, who is four-and-a-half years older, was a student when the school first integrated, but when Lisa got there, "there were always Black kids at school." However, Lisa's memory is that "they would sit off in the back of the room. [...] There was very limited interaction. I never remember a Black student raising their hand to say a thing or I never remember a teacher calling on them." Black students, it seems, were unseen.

It was the early 1960s when Lisa was in elementary school, in the midst of the Civil Rights Movement. Lisa's family attended the local Unitarian Church, whose pastor participated in the Freedom Rides during the summer of 1961, when Black and White civil rights activists organized by the Congress of Racial Equality rode on racially integrated buses across the Deep South. The buses stopped at stations to test the Supreme Court's ruling in *Boynton v. Virginia (1960)*, which held that segregation at interstate bus and rail stations was unconstitutional. Freedom Riders encountered violent resistance across the South, especially in Alabama where Riders were attacked by mobs of White Southerners. Lisa remembers, "There was a lot of talk about civil rights going on in the early '60s and late '50s." She told her parents that she really wanted to participate, but her father's response was, "Don't worry, when you get older there will still be things to do." Hearing this response from her father as a child seemed ludicrous. "How stupid," Lisa thought. "It's going to be solved by then; there won't be anymore problems." Reflecting on this childhood optimism, Lisa pauses and says, "The problems are still here."

Lisa's father passed away when she was just 11 years old. This dramatic change limited her mother's capacity to be as involved in community activism. Up until that time, Lisa had grown up going with her parents to public hearings, Parent Teacher Association (PTA) meetings at school, and doing door-to-door outreach around election season. Meetings were so common for Lisa that when she would play dress-up with her dolls, they would be dressing up to "go to a meeting," not a party or a play date. Without her father around, though, Lisa's mom "went back to work, and she didn't have time to do a lot after that." Thus, when Lisa became "more conscious and aware of what was going on," her mother was less actively involved in the community.

A few years later when Lisa was in high school, she was riding in the car with her mother and her father's political beliefs came up in conversation. "Your father was a socialist, but just don't tell anybody," Mrs. North told Lisa. Though more than a decade removed, the tense memories of McCarthyism were still fresh in Mrs. North's mind. Lisa's father worked as an economist for the federal government and his political affiliations came under close scrutiny during the time when Senator Joseph McCarthy led a nationwide witch hunt ostensibly focused on rooting out Communist influence in the United States. He once received a letter from the government requesting explanation of his affiliation with various organizations. Lisa's parents were afraid that he was going to lose his job and never talked about his socialist convictions because they were scared the wrong people might find out about them.

Whether Lisa knew her father was a socialist, it seems that his influence on her political beliefs was apparent in high school. She took a required 12th-grade class called "Problems in Democracy," which was taught by her favorite teacher. Lisa recalls that one of the most important lessons from the class was her teacher's constant reminder that forms of government and economic systems are actually two different things. Lisa recalls a small group project for which students needed to decide what form of government and what economic system they would want in their ideal country. Her eyes light up when she remembers this activity. Adjusting her glasses and laughing at the memory, she says, "I formed a democratic socialist country. [...] I remember being pretty pushy. I took the lead in the group." The sparkle in her eyes as Lisa tells this story cannot be missed for the connection she is drawing between this high school project and her future activism.

Part II: Union Dues

A key component of Lisa's teacher activism is as a dedicated unionist. She focuses a lot of her efforts toward pushing the United Federation of Teachers (UFT) to be more social justice and community oriented. "There is a bureaucracy up there at the top that they want to maintain and control," she says. "The union doesn't believe in organizing teachers in the school." Lisa's vision of a "much more proactive social justice union" would entail much different behavior on the part of union leadership, including school-based chapter leaders. Rather than focus on maintaining a sense of control and addressing only individual-level concerns, Lisa would have the union be more democratic and action oriented. For Lisa, this means not only more collectively supporting teachers at the school level but also working diligently on larger issues that directly impact the day-to-day experiences of teachers, students, and families across the city.

Lisa first became a union delegate when she taught at PS 20 in the Fort Greene-Clinton Hill neighborhoods of Brooklyn. When a school delegate was elected chapter leader, colleagues encouraged Lisa to fill the open delegate seat. She agreed and started attending Delegate Assembly (DA) meetings to represent her school. The DA is the main UFT decision-making body, which meets monthly to discuss and vote on issues, positions, and policies facing the union as a whole. One chapter leader and a number of delegates based on the size of a school represent each NYC district school in the DA.

It was Lisa's ninth year teaching and it coincided with a change in school leadership. "I think that's when I became really active and aware of the union," Lisa recalls. "Because we had this really horrible principal come in." If teachers spoke up and voiced their opinions during school leadership meetings, the next day administrators would be in their classrooms looking for excuses to write them up. A tense power struggle developed between the principal and the teachers. Teachers started to transfer to other schools and Lisa remembers that within two years, having previously been "the most stable school in District 13," 60 percent of the staff left. The school's chapter leader was one of those who departed and Lisa decided to run for that position. With all the turmoil, her colleagues were happy to elect her. "And that's when I started standing up to the principal," Lisa says, "filing grievances. I had to be very active."

By the time Lisa became chapter leader, she had also made a move to become a Reading Recovery teacher after teaching first grade for eight years. Reading Recovery was a district-based program that placed experienced teachers in schools to support literacy development across classrooms. Lisa partnered with her classroom teacher colleagues to help with reading and literacy instruction, which meant that she did not have her own classroom, but a district administrator, rather than the principal, officially served as her supervisor. "That was one reason I was able to take her [the principal] on," Lisa asserts. "If I had been a classroom teacher at the time, I would have been in big trouble. She couldn't stand it; she realized she couldn't get me."

As chapter leader, Lisa tried turning to the union for help. She called UFT headquarters and asked for support to help protect teachers from unfair treatment at the hands of her principal. The response she received was, "You have enough seniority to transfer." After stressing that it was not herself that she was concerned with, but more so to "make sure things are fair, that they follow the contract and that people have rights," the union officials explained to Lisa that the principal had the support of the district superintendent and there was little they could do. "They wouldn't come in, they wouldn't help," Lisa remembers while shaking her head. "And that's when I started realizing, whoa, the union's not even helping people at the school level. This is an insane, really unfair situation and the union's nowhere. That's what really opened my eyes."

When it was time for her reelection as chapter leader, Lisa found that she had an opponent. The principal had convinced another teacher who was African American to run against Lisa. The school's students and staff were mostly African American, and Lisa suspects the principal thought that would factor in favor of her selected opponent. "She thought I was going to lose that election," Lisa says. The principal started to make plans for the next school year as if Lisa would no longer be chapter leader, but the election was far from a foregone conclusion. "I took the position of standing up to the principal," Lisa explains, "and people voted for me. I won." However, the principal had one more trick up her sleeve. That July, after school was out for the summer, she called Lisa and informed her, "The district has decided that they're not going to have Reading Recovery in our school anymore, so they're going to transfer you to another school." Lisa was furious and spent the whole summer so angry and upset that sometimes she could not sleep. She had enough seniority to stay at her school if she wanted to return as a classroom teacher, but felt that if she did that, then the principal would target her. She also loved being a Reading Recovery teacher and so in the summer of 2000, Lisa accepted a transfer to PS 3, where she has taught since.

Lisa's first experience with labor activism was not as a teacher with the UFT. Her introduction to leftist and labor activism really happened in college and her development as a labor activist sheds light on her approach to work now as a teacher activist. In 1970, Lisa left her hometown for the University of Michigan in Ann Arbor. "Having grown up in the middle of the woods, I was dying to be part of something," she says. Lisa thrust herself into the vast array of political and social movements of the early 1970s, which consumed her early college years. "There was the Vietnam War; we were doing demonstrations," she reflects. "My sister and I got arrested in Washington during the May Day demonstrations of '72." By her sophomore year, she was deeply engaged in the Human Rights Party, a third political party with socialist leanings, which included people active in the gay rights, feminist, and youth movements. "Did I go to school?" she poses rhetorically. "No, I did political stuff."

Working "24 hours a day on the Human Rights Party," Lisa sought out university professors who were also involved and would support independent study credits for her political work. But even as she changed her major to urban studies and was able to get credit for her work with the Party, she started to lose interest in school. She started getting "Cs and Bs and not really paying attention, dropping out of classes." At the end of her sophomore year, Lisa officially took time off from school to do full-time political work and to establish Michigan residency so that she could pay in-state tuition when she returned to school.

In her year off from school, Lisa got a job as a local school bus driver. It was a union job and she became a Teamster. The job introduced her to a lot of local people from neighborhoods in Ann Arbor, not just the university community, but mostly women who worked for the bus company. When she returned to school, a friend from the Human Rights Party helped Lisa land a part-time job doing clerical work in the university's graduate admissions office. The clerical workers had just formed their union when she began working and their members were either students or local women who lived in less expensive areas outside of Ann Arbor.

The union was organized as part of the United Auto Workers (UAW), which was looking to expand its membership base amid auto industry cutbacks in the mid-1970s. At a university with nearly 40,000 students, they represented one of the largest clerical unions in the country. It was so new that it was still working on establishing its local bylaws, and Lisa started working with a more politically active caucus that wanted to draft its own constitution rather than merely adopt what was being handed down from the national UAW. Lisa's group adopted the moniker "Local 2001, The Wave of the Future" and drafted a constitution with "all kinds of democracy written in that the UAW couldn't control." They received pushback from the national leadership when details such as stating that the top salary of a union official could not be higher than the highest paid clerical worker were deemed threatening to the current order. Meetings were filled with shouting matches between members and national UAW representatives who had come to influence the local proceedings. As Wave of the Future members got up to speak, the UAW representatives would try to take the microphone away and then hog the air time trying to convince the local not to elect officers from the upstart caucus who would implement their newly drafted constitution. But Lisa, who was the vice presidential candidate, smiles when she reports, "We won the election, we won the officers." Then, the election committee, which was run by "more UAW kind of people," contested the results, claiming that something was wrong with the election. "So, we re-ran the election and we won again," Lisa remembers triumphantly. "I was the first vice president of Local 2001, The Wave of the Future."

In an interesting turn of events, the forces aligned against the Wave of the Future platform sought to decertify the union, and Lisa and her colleagues found themselves engaged in a new battle. Lisa's group of "political people" were "mostly regular clericals" and mostly "all women." But, there was also a young man who was helping them fight back against the decertification campaign. His "parents were kind of political" and he was a former member of the Spartacist League, a left-wing Trotskyist offshoot of the larger Youth Socialist Movement. Lisa butted heads with the ex-Spartacist. "We would put out fliers that said, 'the running dog capitalist bureaucrats,'" Lisa describes. Concerned that such strident language would not resonate with her coworkers, many of whom were wives of farmers or autoworkers, Lisa said, "You can say the same kind of thing, but you don't have to use that terminology." "Oh no! We have to use that," her new male colleague responded. "They have to get used it." Citing the lack of connection her team was making with the majority of union members, Lisa shakes her head as she recalls, "And so, the union was basically decertified by five votes."

The lessons Lisa learned from her labor activist efforts in college have stuck with her. Related to how her clerical coworkers were not finding the unionizing efforts to be relevant enough to their everyday challenges, Lisa talks to a lot of other teachers who "see things that are wrong and don't particularly like a lot of things and like to complain so much. At this point in time, teachers are pretty apathetic. They love to complain, complain, complain. The union doesn't do this. The union doesn't do that." These sentiments from teachers are what motivate Lisa to push for the UFT to be more social justice oriented and to identify issues around which it can organize teachers in schools. Lisa believes that there are certain issues that will motivate teachers to take a more active role in trying to effect change. "So for me," she continues, "I am always trying to think, 'Well, what are the issues that teachers seem willing to move on? What are the issues that teachers will come together and say we are willing to do something about this and then figure out how to do it?'"

It is not as if there is a shortage of issues. There is not a meeting I have with Lisa when she does not refer to and then find and give to me some piece of literature—news articles, pamphlets, event fliers, petitions—expounding upon an important education justice issue. She does so after rummaging in her bag, an overflowing backpack stuffed with these papers along with classroom teaching resources. Whatever does not fit in her backpack can be found in the backseat of her car, which is home to various folders with piles of newsletters and fliers ready for distribution. The materials contain information about a whole host of issues facing the U.S. education system: mayoral control of school systems, teacher evaluation and merit pay, high-stakes testing, school closings, charter schools, growing class sizes, and increasingly rigid and mandated curricula.

If their unions are not providing adequate activist space for teachers to take on education justice issues, then teacher activists must find alternative venues for their work. Thus, in addition to being active in the union, Lisa is engaged with NYCoRE and a newer group called the Grassroots Education Movement (GEM). I attend a GEM monthly members meeting with Lisa at the City University of New York (CUNY) Grad Center in March 2011. The room is set up with long tables pushed together to form a large rectangle with chairs lining the outer edges. A second row of chairs lines the wall behind the main table and I choose to sit there, not wanting to take up space in the center. The seats fill quickly as people arrive and soon every chair is occupied. There are more than 40 people in attendance, and as they introduce themselves they share where and what they teach. The group represents a mixture of teaching experience ranging from early childhood to high school levels, and teachers in their first year to veterans and retirees.

Lisa sits at the end of the table nearest the entryway and she cofacilitates the meeting. The heart of this meeting is hearing from a guest, Rafael Feliciano, who is the president of the Federacion de Maestros de Puerto Rico (FMPR), the Puerto Rican teachers' union. He has been part of a long-term struggle in Puerto Rico to establish the kind of union and teacher activism that Lisa envisions in NYC. His talk echoes many of the themes and ideas that Lisa has shared with me during our time together.

Rafi, as he is more commonly known, recounts how his more progressive faction of the union gained power, and how the union has gained the support of the general public in Puerto Rico. He starts in 1971, when the Socialist Workers caucus began its work inside schools, not inside the union. At individual schools, the caucus was able to create more open spaces for debate and bring together different ideas. Rafi also notes that because teachers in Puerto Rico are, by and large, members of the communities in which they teach and earn similar salaries to other workers, forming alliances with parents around school-based and education issues is more organic. Lisa has discussed with me the challenge of teachers living relatively far from the communities in which they teach. "I think if the teachers were more from the communities—and you don't have to be from the community but have a community focus—if the expectation of teachers was that when you come into the school you become part of that community and not just a sense of, 'I am teaching the kids and I am doing my job and I leave.' If there was a different kind of expectation, I think it would be much more powerful here in this country," Lisa explained in one of our interviews.

According to Rafi, the Puerto Rican teachers held themselves to the level of community accountability and solidarity Lisa talks about. Specifically, they did not start their fight around salary issues; instead, they fought for better school facilities, special education, books, and materials. After solidifying their relationships with communities, Rafi's caucus made a strong effort to build leadership within the union from the bottom up. Soon, the caucus was able to influence the FMPR so that it put resources behind school-based struggles. Some boycotted tests, others lobbied for more resources or improved facilities, and some even decided to strike over issues like these in spite of Puerto Rico's law prohibiting teachers from striking. Rafi stresses that they were able to take radical actions because they were done in solidarity with parents and the communities were behind them.

When Rafi finishes talking, there is time for discussion and the GEM teachers who have been listening intently start right in. A GEM member asks, "How did you boycott the test? Tell us how to do that!" Rafi's answer is simple and plain: They had parent petitions, parents and students were part of the campaign from the beginning, and it was not an imposition on the part of teachers. The centrality of parent voice and community power to Rafi's story of *teacher* struggle is striking. At this moment, Lisa speaks up after having quietly listened to Rafi's story and the few questions and answers offered thus far. As she talks, she steals a glance in my direction as if to make sure that I am listening.

"The key is an alliance between parents and teachers," she tells her GEM colleagues, her voice rising to drive home the importance of her point. "New York has a history of separation between teachers and parents, and we have to form alliances between teachers, parents, and students *over time*. When the grassroots takes control of the union, *that's* the direction we have to go." Her belief in the need for the UFT to be driven by the issues and needs that will be relevant to members coincides with her belief in the need for an alliance between parents and teachers. In fact, her experience as a parent activist is actually the major reason Lisa became a teacher in the first place. As a result, Lisa's teacher activist work not only includes a vision of a teachers' union that pays its dues to the everyday needs of parents and the community but also includes doing activist work directly with parent organizing groups.

Part III: Parent Power

After losing the clerical union fight at the University of Michigan, Lisa left school without graduating and returned to the East Coast. She became involved in a committed relationship with another woman, and Lisa and her partner bounced around between New York and Baltimore for a couple of years before settling down in 1978 in South Richmond Hill, a close-knit "mostly Puerto Rican and West Indian" community in Queens, New York. Still interested in union activism, she got a job driving delivery trucks—the second woman ever hired to deliver Hostess Cakes in New York. It was a Teamster union job and she quickly found and joined a group, Teamsters for a Democratic Union (TDU). TDU is a grassroots organization of Teamster members dedicated to "uniting Teamsters to put our union to work for the members."[1] As an independent group of rank-and-file union members, TDU organizes members to "fight for good contracts and oppose concessions and benefit cuts" and "to hold union officials accountable to the members." She eventually left Hostess for a higher-paying job delivering Entenmann's cakes and continued doing organizing with TDU. But when talking about her first decade in NYC, Lisa does not share too much about her work with TDU. Instead, she recalls more about her family and neighborhood in Queens.

Lisa's partner, who was Puerto Rican, had a son who was just starting school when they moved to New York and they "got very involved in the community." Block associations kept people connected and there were a lot of young families whose kids played together on the streets, "running in each other's houses," creating the sense that everyone was "taking care of each other's kids." Like her own parents, Lisa and her partner got involved in the elementary school's Parents' Association. In fact, Lisa's partner became president. At the same time, Lisa stopped working for Entenmann's to have a baby and, after her son was born, she decided not to go back to work right away. She volunteered at the school during the day, tutored children in the neighborhood, and started to notice some disturbing patterns. "I knew all the kids," Lisa reflects. "They would start going to school and then they would start failing, not doing well in kindergarten, first grade. They were struggling with school." From her tutoring, Lisa knew that all "the kids wanted to succeed" and she also knew that the families in her neighborhood believed that education "was extremely important." She began to ask herself, "What was going on?"

Getting more involved with the Parents' Association, Lisa started to learn more about educational inequities across different neighborhoods in the local school district. District 28 included the comfortably middle- and upper middle-class area of Forest Hills along with the more working class and low-income areas of South Richmond Hill, South Ozone Park, and South Jamaica. Forest Hills schools always seemed to have nicer buildings and facilities, while the school where Lisa's partner's child attended in South Ozone Park had a leaky roof and was in general disrepair. In addition, most of the teachers were White and lived in middle-class communities in Long Island; they lacked the perspective and relationships to connect with the largely low-income families of color in the school.

As a gay parent, Lisa knew first hand how it felt to be marginalized by the public schools. "You don't want things taken out on your kid," Lisa remembers, fearing that a teacher or school administrator's prejudices might negatively affect the way her son would be treated. She and her partner "wouldn't say we were gay; we just said we're both raising him." During her son's kindergarten year, Lisa and her partner broke up and began living separately. At the time, her son had a class assignment to draw a self-portrait. When he was finished, he took a black crayon and scribbled bold, dark lines scratching out his picture. His teacher asked Lisa to come in and talk about why her son might have scribbled over his own portrait. Lisa explained:

> "His whole life up until now, we have been living with a friend who has helped raise him and she's not there anymore."
> "Well, does she still see him?" the teacher asked.
> "Yeah, they still see each other," answered Lisa.
> "Well then, there's no problem," the teacher declared.

"She didn't get it at all, and I didn't feel comfortable enough with my situation to explain," Lisa recalls. She felt vulnerable, unsure about how this teacher—who was not reading between the lines—might react to knowing that Lisa was gay.

Lisa "understood how parents felt coming as an 'other' into the school system and not feeling supported" and worked with the Parents' Association to organize fellow parents to have more of a say in their children's education. The Parents' Association started to hold meetings to talk about important issues and to learn about different topics in education. Partnering with a local

university, the Association planned workshop sessions about different learning styles for teachers and parents together and would "fill up huge rooms."
The Parents' Association started gaining traction and instituted a newsletter
in which local businesses could take out small ads. "We really started building
this whole community," Lisa remembers. "And for a lot of parents in the community, it was really an exciting time."

Soon Lisa was ready to reenter the workforce, but was not interested in
waking up at three or four in the morning to deliver Entenmann's cakes now
that she had a child. Instead, Lisa's engagement in schools as a parent led her
to consider becoming a teacher. Lisa still had lingering questions about the
way schools were working: "What is going on here? There are these kids who
are so excited about learning, but they are not making it. Is there something
wrong with the way education is?" These questions challenged Lisa to think,
"Well, maybe I should figure that out. I never thought about being a teacher
until then." Becoming a teacher meant that Lisa would have to finish her
undergraduate degree. She called the University of Michigan and found out
that she could finish her remaining coursework at a local college and transfer the credits. After completing her undergraduate degree requirements,
Lisa enrolled in a teacher credential program. In 1989, with a newly minted
teacher certification, she landed her first teaching job at PS 20.

As much as her teacher activist work has focused on the union, Lisa's passion also lies with her vision for bringing parents and teachers together. She
has a vision for what parent-teacher solidarity might look like:

> I have been saying this for a long time, that what if the New York City Teachers'
> Union says on May 6th, for instance, when the weather is not too bad, we are going
> into the middle of Manhattan and we are going to have a demonstration and we are
> going to sit down and we are not going home. Now this will take a lot of organizing. It
> is not something that is going to happen immediately, but you get as many parents as
> you can on board for this and all the advocacy groups in the city to join you. It is not
> to say that you wouldn't be deluged with all the antiunion stuff, but you sit down in
> the middle of the city and you say, "Until these schools get the money they need and
> the kind of education kids deserve, we are not going anywhere." If 100,000 teachers
> sat down in the middle of Manhattan and hopefully another 20,000 or 30,000 par-
> ents, we would have the kind of education much closer to the kind of education that
> the kids of New York City deserve.

Lisa chuckles to herself as she paints a picture of what would probably be the
biggest demonstration for public education in New York's history. There is
a mixture of hope and disbelief in her voice. Her idea seems so simple, yet

nearly impossible. Her disbelief stems from her sense that the sheer magnitude of what she suggests might be necessary to actually secure the "kind of education that the kids of New York City deserve." Her hope, though, is rooted in the solidarity work she does with parents in the interim as a member of the NYC Coalition for Educational Justice (CEJ).

During the late 1990s, stemming from successful grassroots organizing efforts in the South Bronx, parent activism and organizing started to increase around NYC public schools. When the NYC schools came under mayoral control in 2002, centralizing the most important decision making with the mayor's office and his appointed chancellor, a collection of outer borough— the Bronx, Brooklyn, and Queens—parent organizing groups realized that they needed to build a citywide powerbase to have influence in this new system of governance. They came together in 2006 to form CEJ. CEJ's mission to end the inequity of resources and outcomes across the city's schools resonated with Lisa's own history of activism as a parent in Queens.

CEJ meets monthly at the Annenberg Institute for School Reform offices in the Woolworth Building in downtown Manhattan. As we wait for the elevators in the large foyer, Lisa and I admire the meticulously detailed architecture and design. Gold-leafed designs line the cathedral ceilings in the foyer above the elevators. It is an amazingly beautiful building, a symbol of the long-standing corporate wealth that drives so much of New York's prominence in the world. It feels ironic that we are going to a meeting of mostly low-income parents of color who have traveled from very different communities in the Bronx, Brooklyn, and Queens to be there. As powerful corporate executives enter similarly majestic buildings across the city, CEJ parents and organizers arrive to empower those who are usually kept out of such spaces.

CEJ gathers in the large meeting room in the center of the Annenberg office suite. The tables are removed and the room's perimeter is lined with chairs that are packed as tightly as possible. Nearly 50 people are present; every chair is taken and people are sitting on the floor as well standing crowded by the double doors that remain open so they can see and hear what is happening. There is an English/Spanish interpreter who is speaking into a microphone that sends her voice to headsets worn by about half of the participants, both English and Spanish speakers, so that they can understand each other with simultaneous translation.

When we arrive, we are greeted warmly; everyone recognizes Lisa right away, and they accept me by association. I am immediately reminded of a previous conversation with Lisa when she described CEJ as warm, nice, friendly, and family-like, and that there is always good food and good people. People hug each other hello and there is time carved out in meeting agendas for relationships to grow. Lisa squeezes in past those crowded at the doorway and sits down on the floor. Even though CEJ is primarily for parent activists, Lisa is part of the coalition through the UFT Brooklyn Parent Outreach Committee. In an effort to forge stronger ties with parents, the UFT has a Parent Outreach Committee in every borough staffed by a Parent and Community Liaison. The Brooklyn liaison has played a particularly active role in connecting parent leaders to citywide education organizing efforts, which is how Brooklyn Parent Outreach became a CEJ member organization.

The meeting is already underway and the group is engaged in a conversation about trying to set campaign priorities that are citywide, but that also resonate with their local communities. Each of the member organizations has a constituency to which it is accountable locally and in order to motivate and mobilize people around citywide work, the issues must be relevant across neighborhoods. As the discussion identifies possible topics that have citywide impact, Lisa raises the issue of connecting teachers with communities and families. She mentions that the UFT has passed a resolution decrying the "disappearance of Black and Latino teachers." An organizer chimes in to talk about Chicago's "Grow Your Own Teacher" efforts to train and support parents of color to become teachers in Chicago Public Schools. Other issues are raised, including public school budgets, school closings, and even the presence of PCBs, a toxic chemical found in many school lighting fixtures. Toward the end of the meeting, there are reminders of a few different dates—one for a discussion about teacher seniority rights that is being hosted by the union and another for a hearing for those who were arrested at a recent civil disobedience action protesting school closures. As an observer, I feel a bit overwhelmed with the broad scope of the discussion. As powerful as the group feels, and as much energy as there is around citywide change, this brainstorming session seems to span far and wide, and it is not clear to me where and how a group like CEJ should focus. Nevertheless, the meeting ends with a powerfully unifying cheer, successively in English and Spanish, call and response: "Who are we!?" "C-E-J!" "Quienes somos!?" "C-E-J!"

For Lisa, her purpose for being part of CEJ is to connect with parent organizations as a teacher activist and as someone active within the UFT. But there are challenges in connecting these two constituencies. GEM, for instance, is largely made up of White leftists; older, longtime union and labor activists; younger White teachers; and just a handful of people of color. This reflects the racial demographic of the broader teaching force, but stands in stark contrast to the students and communities of color that the NYC public schools predominantly serve. CEJ, on the other hand, is almost entirely made up of people of color, parents of public school students throughout NYC along with a handful of White teacher allies and White staff members. The meetings are led by parents and in two languages, English and Spanish. Within both groups, there is a sense of community, shared perspective, and solidarity. But for CEJ, there is common understanding of what it means to struggle as a parent of color in a place like New York and what the real consequences are for children caught in a failing school system. For a teacher like Lisa—White and relatively privileged as someone earning a middle-class salary—to commit to CEJ is powerful. She could choose, as do many of her colleagues, not to engage, but she believes that change will not happen in schools without parents and teachers working together, and as she has said to me before, "CEJ is where parents are, and so that's where teachers should be too."

Part IV: Dealing with Disconnection

Lisa's activist journey started in her youth in the 1960s—a decade when the relationship between the NYC teachers' union and parents and community members was slowly deteriorating. In 1968, the union backed away from its initial support for "community control" at schools in Ocean Hill-Brownsville, Brooklyn, and Harlem. The UFT went on strike in protest of the "community control" experiment, which was designed to give Black communities more say in how their schools were being run. Ever since, the distrust and disunity between the UFT and New York's communities of color has been difficult to overcome. Despite Lisa's efforts to connect her activist work with teachers and parents, she laments at what she sees as "a disconnect" between the two groups. "Teachers love to blame parents," Lisa reflects. "It is scary how anti-parent a lot of teachers are and the union also doesn't do anything to change that." Even in her own school, Lisa hears negative attitudes from her teacher colleagues about parents. She wishes there were more critical conversations about parent involvement: "I mean, what can we do about parents not being involved with their kids' education? What can we do to try and change this? What can we do to bring in a few more parents? That conversation never exists." At her school, it is easy for Lisa to feel alone in her efforts to connect with parents.

My final visit to see Lisa underscores her isolation when I attend a Brooklyn District 13 Community Education Council (CEC) meeting held at the school on a Saturday morning. A warm sunny morning greets me when I arrive at the front entrance of PS 3 and see a sign posted directing visitors to the other side of the building closer to the auditorium. I walk around the building, strolling through the park adjacent to the school, and make my way inside. At a table just past the entryway sit a security guard and a woman making additional signs to post for others who might not know their way around to the auditorium entrance. I recognize the woman as a parent leader from *The Inconvenient Truth Behind Waiting for Superman*—a GEM film produced in response to *Waiting for Superman*, a controversial documentary that celebrates charter schools and vilifies teachers and their unions. GEM's film title is an ironic twist on the fact that Davis Guggenheim was the filmmaker behind both *An Inconvenient Truth*, a documentary about global warming and climate change, and *Waiting for Superman*. GEM seeks to dismantle the arguments put forward in *Waiting for Superman* by sharing the experiences of parents and teachers in NYC who are disillusioned with charter schools and promote the promise of district public schools. Lisa has told me that PS 3 is facing competition from new charter schools in Bedford-Stuyvesant that are sending out glossy promotional materials and buying ad space in the local subway stations to recruit families away from the district public schools. Already faced with enough challenges, Lisa's school diverts much-needed resources to recruitment activities in order to maintain level enrollment. The event would seem a good opportunity for PS 3 faculty and administration to strengthen their ties with local families. However, Lisa is on her own this morning; she is the only teacher present.

Today, the District 13 CEC plans to screen *The Inconvenient Truth Behind Waiting for Superman*, followed by a panel of parents and teachers featured in the film, and finishing with a community barbecue. I introduce myself to the woman I recognize and tell her that I am a friend of Lisa's. Her name is Khem and she is a PS 3 parent and a CEC representative. Khem explains the history behind the CEC structure. In 2002, New York State passed the legislation for mayoral control, and it also got rid of the 32 community school boards in NYC. The CECs were created in place of the community school boards and PTA officers at each school within a district elect the nine CEC members. While the argument was that the CECs would make the mayor accountable to the community, in Khem's opinion, this has not happened. The mayor controls the funds that come to the CECs and all they have power over are district zoning lines and trying to help schools raise additional resources.

When I arrive, only two families are present, but it strikes me that entire families are attending this meeting. The other meetings I have attended with Lisa have not been family-friendly environments. This meeting is not in a tall office building in Manhattan; it is at a neighborhood school in a residential community surrounded by row houses and brownstones next to the community playground. Sure enough, as more people start filtering in, most are parents with children in tow.

Lisa is running around greeting families and helping get things prepared. She moves through the auditorium, stopping to hand out PS 3 summer arts program brochures and encouraging families to consider signing up their children. After she speaks to every family, she moves off behind the stage to make sure the microphones are set up and turned on. Even though she is not the one organizing this event, she still uses the opportunity to search for and build connections, and she is there to support Khem as a parent leader who has done most of the planning for today. Khem gets things started by moving to the front of the stage and calling for everyone's attention. "PS 3 is one of the oldest schools in New York City," she says. "It is also the largest elementary school in District 13." Khem runs down a list of programs that PS 3 has for its children and families and talks about the partnerships the school has with community-based organizations to maintain the presence of the arts and music in the building. Many schools in District 13 have had to cut their music and arts programs due to budget constraints and Khem encourages other parents to find out how to build partnerships with community-based organizations at their schools too.

Lisa chimes in that they also have a school-community garden starting up. "We have already built the beds but are waiting for the soil to be delivered," she explains. "You can see the beds outside the school nestled between the school and the park." Khem uses Lisa's participation as a bridge to talk about the importance of building parent-teacher partnerships. "Teachers are with our kids for six to seven hours a day," she says. "As parents, we need to make sure that we are communicating with teachers and partnering with them to make sure our children are getting the education that they deserve." Next, Khem notes that the current mayoral control legislation sunsets in 2014. "I don't support mayoral control," she states. "I don't believe that any of Bloomberg's chancellor appointments have been qualified to run our school system. We need to rally behind our legislators to think of a new system for NYC. We are the parents and we should have the most say about what should happen in our schools."

After a brief student awards ceremony that recognizes students from each of the District 13 elementary schools for excellent attendance and academic achievement, the film screening is ready to begin. In the crowd of about 40 people, a little less than half are children. The film is about an hour long and the crowd thins out a bit by the end, many of the children having found their way to the playground next to the school. After the film is over, there is time for a Q&A session with the three panelists: Julie, a teacher, GEM leader, and one of the film's narrators; Mae, a parent who is featured in the film and formerly had her children enrolled at an Achievement First charter school in Brooklyn; and Jae, a parent who is also in the film whose child was denied a seat at a Harlem Success Academy charter school because it could not accommodate her special-education needs. Khem serves as the moderator. Her husband has fired up the grills outside and the smell of the warming charcoals is wafting through the windows, a reminder for those who stick around that their reward will be some food once the Q&A session is complete.

One question is from a father who asks if they had a magic wand, what change would they make? Khem lists a bunch of things she would like to change: that schools embrace all cultures, that they build everything around children, they pay attention to the arts, that there is more teacher autonomy around curricula and pedagogy. Julie says she would like to shut down the centralized Department of Education and establish a system and schools that are directly responsive to communities and the responsibility of communities—so that schools are open 12 hours a day and teachers, parents, and administrators are working together to make decisions. Jae says we need more civic and community engagement and suggests mandatory requirements for civic engagement in classrooms and that assessments should be used to distribute support, not shut down schools. Mae answers that she would want special-education children to be cared for, taught well, and have their needs met, along with counseling for families about how to support special-needs children.

When Mae is finished and the microphone is being passed back to Khem in order to field the next question, Lisa strides across the front of the stage to intercept it. There is urgency in her steps, lending some weight to whatever she is about to say. She starts by saying that high-stakes tests are "deforming public education." "Teachers are so preoccupied with tests that it impacts the ways they teach," she continues. "They cut out field trips where students can get out into the community. We no longer have structured learning by doing and playing—even when it's especially important at the lower elementary school grades. Ultimately, because of the tests, teachers can't deliver the curriculum they want to teach." Lisa has talked to me about these issues before and sees testing as a place where teachers and parents might unite. However,

I again have a sense of being overwhelmed by the vast array of challenges being raised without a clear course of action for moving forward.

There are a few more spirited exchanges in response to audience questions, and Khem brings the Q&A session to a close by declaring to a round of applause, "We need to make sure that parents and teachers are empowered to work together!" We move out of the auditorium and follow our noses toward the grills outside. There, we find steaming hot trays filled with cooked chicken, hot dogs, hamburgers, beans and white rice, and people help themselves to the makeshift buffet. The smell of food has also attracted more families from the neighborhood and the crowd outside is bigger than the one that just finished watching the film. Some people take their food back inside to the cafeteria where clusters of parents are eating together, engaged in conversation about schools, parenting, and more.

I look over at Lisa who is smiling, obviously happy to be there. She is enjoying the opportunity to sit and talk with parents about what needs to happen to improve their schools. Instead of seeming overwhelmed, she looks calmly satisfied. I realize that for her, this is just one of many meetings and events. For now, she may not be doing this with 100,000 teachers—in fact, it is just her this morning—and there are just about 20–30 parents in attendance, not 20,000–30,000. They won't be shutting down midtown Manhattan anytime soon. But wherever she is, Lisa is searching for the connections, listening for the issues that will continue bringing people together, and hoping that one of these days she will be able to look around and smile at the thousands of teachers and parents who will have gathered together in solidarity to demand the schools that NYC children deserve.

Part V: Reflections on Building Solidarity

Lisa's teacher activism is a project in building solidarity. Her biography is one of seeking to work with others to right wrongs and create a better society. As a second-grader, though she was too young, she wanted to go on Freedom Rides with civil rights activists, and in college she started to make connections between her increasingly radical politics and labor activism. For labor activists, the concept of solidarity is important. The rallying cry, "Workers of the world, unite!" is a paraphrase of the final line in Marx and Engels's (1848) hugely influential *Communist Manifesto*. The English translation of this line is actually, "Working men [sic] of all countries, unite!" and conveys the explicit sense of international solidarity that Marx and Engels called for in a revolutionary socialist movement. In the case of revolutionary socialism, the underlying principle of solidarity among workers is based on the assertion of their shared interests as those oppressed by the prevailing economic system, regardless of where they lived. Lisa seeks to build solidarity between parents and teachers based on what she sees as their shared interests as key stakeholders in the potential for schools and education to change the world around them.

As a parent, Lisa experienced the power and promise of parents working together to build connections with their neighborhood schools. As a teacher, she sees the factors that limit what teachers can accomplish in their classrooms, but also identifies a strong disconnect between teachers and families as a significant obstacle in fighting for change. As a teacher activist, whenever she gets the chance, Lisa's message is clear: "Parents and teachers of the world, unite!" From the excitement she displayed at the GEM meeting for the FMPR's strategy of connecting with parents and community members before it took on any militant labor actions to her own experience as a parent who advocated for improvements at her child's school, Lisa believes that "the key is an alliance between parents and teachers." However, even as Lisa admits, the kind of solidarity she envisions between parents and teachers is not something for which she sees enough teachers striving.

Freire wrote extensively about the concept of solidarity. His work seems especially important for urban teacher activists in the United States where urban school teachers are often not members of the communities they serve. As members of a relatively privileged class (earning middle-class salaries and possessing high levels of education), Marxist sensibilities of solidarity may not ring true for teachers serving low-income communities of color. Instead, they need to develop a Freirean sense of solidarity, which "requires that one enter into the situation of those with whom one is solidary [...] fighting at their side to transform the objective reality" (Freire, 1993, pp. 31–32).

Lisa's solidarity with the communities she serves has developed from her own experiences that have removed any abstraction in her mind regarding the nature of oppression. The neighborhood kids in South Richmond Hill whom Lisa watched enter school excited to learn only to return with feelings of failure and dejection were dealt with unjustly. Lisa understands how parents feel when deprived of their voice because this is how she felt as a lesbian mother who was worried that homophobic prejudice might get "taken out on your kid." These moments in Lisa's life enable her to work in true solidarity with parents, "fighting at their side," as Freire urges.

Her challenge to teachers, then, is to think about how their work is based on the Freirean values of solidarity. If it is Lisa's biographical journey that resonates in her work with parents and teachers, then other teacher activists need to reflect upon the moments in their own lives when they can recognize oppression. It may be their personal experiences or their bearing witness to others', but these moments must be drawn upon if they are to build solidarity in the face of injustice.

Note

1. TDU descriptions taken from http://www.tdu.org/ (retrieved May 11, 2013).

References

Freire, P. (1993). *Pedagogy of the oppressed*. New York: Continuum.

Marx, K. & Engels, F. (1848). *Manifesto of the Communist party*. In R.C. Tucker (ed.), *The Marx-Engels Reader* (2nd ed.) (pp. 473–500). New York: W.W. Norton & Company.

THE PEDAGOGY OF TEACHER ACTIVISM: PURPOSE, POWER, AND POSSIBILITY

I can go no further in this book without acknowledging an underlying tension between me, the portraitist, and Rosie, Natalia, Kari, and Lisa, the protagonists. I identify as a man, they as women. My positionality as a male raised in a patriarchal society has led me, at times, to question the legitimacy of my assuming the role of portraitist for four female teacher activists. It seems no mere coincidence that my mind bends toward critical education theorists who are predominantly male (Paulo Freire, Henry Giroux, Peter McLaren, Bill Ayers, Jeff Duncan-Andrade, etc.). The first draft of this final chapter almost exclusively cited the work of the male scholars listed above. As valuable as their contributions have been, sole reliance on their theoretical precedents are inadequate to the task of positing the pedagogy of teacher activism, especially when drawing lessons from the lives and work of four female protagonists. For this, and in all efforts to deepen understanding about teaching and education, I must also turn to critical feminist education scholars such as Gloria Anzaldúa, Lilia Bartolomé, Patricia Hill Collins, Antonia Darder, Madeline Grumet, bell hooks, and more. The pedagogy of teacher activism outlined in this final chapter represents my best thinking, as a male, about what we can all learn by listening to lessons taught primarily by women.

As raised previously in this book, early social reproduction theories were applied to schools in overly deterministic fashion, casting teachers and students as passive objects caught in the inevitable replication of unequal social order. Importantly, Grumet's (1988) work on women and teaching reclaims the procreative function of human reproduction to lay the groundwork for analyzing curriculum and pedagogy through a womanist lens. Through this lens, Grumet (1988) works to "recover the reproductive projects" of women teaching to find "the intentionality contained in their pedagogy" (p. 47). Reframing the meaning of reproduction as focused on procreative activity casts illuminating light on Freire's (in Hermance, 2012) statement, "No one is born fully-formed: it is through self-experience in the world that we become what we are" (p. 2). As the teacher activists in this book show us, they were not born ready to do the work that they do. By mining their biographical histories and trajectories of political development, we more fully understand how they each procreatively became teacher activists whose work centers the cultivation of a more just human society.

As a reminder, this is not a teaching methods book. It is a book about pedagogy. There is a difference. Attempts to codify teaching practices into step-by-step methodologies oversimplify the nuanced work of education. Reformers searching for technical solutions to the challenges of education look for methodological approaches that prescribe particular, often rigid, teaching practices, overlooking the routinely ambiguous and dialectical nature of human action. However, Grumet (1988) stressed the importance of "body knowledge," pedagogy that stems from lived experience and life history, which are often sidelined by masculine epistemologies focused on mechanistic predictability and control. Additionally, treating teaching merely as a technical enterprise obfuscates the sociocultural and political realities that give rise and shape to the challenges that many educators seek to address (Bartolomé, 1994; Giroux, 1992; Simmons, 2013). I am not interested in codifying a *methodology* of teacher activism, rather I seek to understand the *pedagogy* that undergirds the work.

Pedagogy refers to the conceptual ethos that surrounds the practice of teaching. Teachers might be sound methodologically, but if they lack pedagogy, then they risk teaching without purpose and direction. For teacher activists, pedagogy is articulated through a commitment to education as a practice of freedom and possibility and the creation of a new just world. A commitment to bring a new world into being implicates life experiences as mothers (and fathers) and daughters (and sons), which provide literal and metaphorical reference points to projects of procreation and reproduction

(Grumet, 1988). This commitment also leads teacher activists to honor the complex personal and political realities of teaching and learning by engaging in critical dialogue and reflection focused on issues of power, agency, morality, democracy, justice, and change (Giroux, 2007). Through these lenses, we can more fully see teaching and pedagogy by breaking down the barriers erected by dominant educational theories that obstruct the public from private in our creation of culture and consciousness. Therefore, an effort to understand the pedagogy of teacher activism rests upon the exploration of why and how teacher activists ground their praxis in private and public arenas.

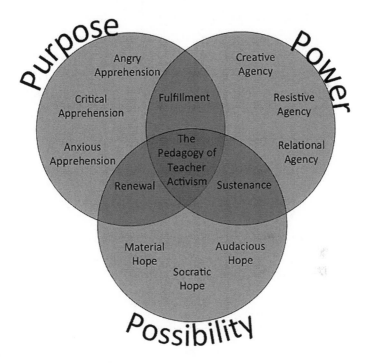

Figure 1. **The Pedagogy of Teacher Activism.** This diagram depicts the lessons of purpose, power, and possibility that comprise the pedagogy of teacher activism.
Source: Author.

This final chapter explores three lessons in pedagogy taught by our protagonists' stories of becoming and being teacher activists: purpose, power, and possibility (see Figure 1). First, I will examine how the development of purpose drew Rosie, Natalia, Kari, and Lisa into the work of teacher activism and provides ongoing motivation for their actions. Next, I analyze their work as attempts to challenge and shift power relations. Finally, it is a sense of possibility and hope that helps frame their work so that it may continue, even in the face of seeming impossibility. I conclude by offering brief thoughts about current trends in education reform as they relate to the pedagogy of teacher activism and what many in the field of education might do to support the promise of teacher activism.

Purpose: Lessons of Apprehension

The word "apprehension" has multiple meanings: (1) anxiety or fear that something bad or unpleasant will happen and (2) understanding; grasp (Oxford Dictionaries, n.d.). In becoming teacher activists, Rosie, Natalia, Kari, and Lisa each experience sharp moments of apprehension about their realities. These moments often start out as anxiety-inducing, but then lead to a deeper understanding from which they derive and drive their purpose for teacher activism.

With respect to her queer identity, Rosie experienced anxious apprehension at an early age. In kindergarten and first grade, Rosie remembers liking girls. She would tell people openly that she liked girls, but then remembers, "in second grade knowing that I shouldn't talk about it, knowing that it was wrong." She went into the closet until she was 17 years old, but believes that being told "it was wrong" to acknowledge and follow her natural feelings helped her later understanding that the world is "not the way everyone tells it to you."

Reinforcing her sense that the world is "not the way everyone tells it," Rosie saw hypocrisy in the ways that dominant institutions behaved. For example, in college, administrators displayed disparate treatment of student efforts to establish a Gay-Straight Alliance (GSA) and the hyper-heterosexualized activities of fraternities. Their tacit support for the fraternities, coupled with an outright denial of students' wishes for a GSA, drove Rosie's desire to become an activist to expose such inconsistencies. In the words of Edward Said (in Giroux, 2007), she learned "to temper any reverence for authority with a sense of critical awareness" (p. 1). Her distrust of dominant worldviews precipitated her purpose to expose privilege and power.

Kari's purpose was derived from an early "interest in wanting to change things, or feeling like the system was not fair" because of her family's history of being sent to Japanese American internment camps during WWII. Reflecting on how she might feel if she were not Japanese American, Kari says, "I may not feel that way about the government, about the system, simply because I wouldn't have had that experience in my family." Her family's history engendered a distrust and anxious skepticism about "the system," and then her educational experiences strengthened her feelings that "the system was not fair."

Kari's first teaching experience as a 22-year-old fresh out of college was teaching a remedial prealgebra class, which had "all students of color," many of whom Kari thought "shouldn't have been there." Kari believed, "they should have been in a regular or an advanced class, but they had emotional or behavioral issues." The calculus taught in the same classroom by a different teacher "was mostly White students," reflective of her high school experience where honors classes had disproportionately high numbers of White students. Now, Kari makes sure that she teaches AP Calculus to the students at her school, who are almost entirely low-income students of color.

While Rosie's purpose works to expose the system for its unjust reality and to empower marginalized identities, Kari's focus as a teacher activist is trained on trying to subvert the system by providing access to those who are typically excluded. For Kari's teacher activism, rigorous math acts as a stand-in for the system. She does not question the power and privilege afforded to high-level math knowledge, but instead her understanding of the system leads her to ensure that students like those she has seen excluded from high-level math classes in the past are afforded access.

Lisa and Natalia both also had experiences that exposed them to the unjust reality of schools and society. For Lisa, already a seasoned political and labor activist, it was her experience as a parent that provided her with purpose as a teacher. While she stayed at home to care for her infant son, she volunteered at the local school and also tutored children from her neighborhood. Her knowledge of the neighborhood children as eager learners who "wanted to succeed" was inconsistent with their experience when they went to school only to "start failing." Lisa knew that families in her neighborhood believed that education was "extremely important" and she sensed that something was wrong with the school system, not understanding why there was such dissonance between what she knew about neighborhood families compared to their children's experiences in school.

This experience motivated Lisa to get more involved as a parent activist. "The work I did in the Parents' Association when my stepson, my partner, and I were living in Queens and she was the president of the Parents' Association—that is when I decided," Lisa reflects about her decision to become a teacher. "I never thought about being a teacher until then and I think I saw that parents can organize and have an effect on what is happening." Furthermore,

Lisa's apprehensive feelings as a gay parent gave her an understanding of what it means for parents to be distrustful and fearful of teachers and schools, feelings that are all too common for families who are excluded from dominant schooling practices on the basis of race, class, gender, religion, sexuality, or any other marker of social oppression. Based on these experiences as a parent, Lisa finds purpose in working to bring parents and teachers together to improve schools.

Growing up with an immigrant Latina mom revealed to Natalia ways in which U.S. society unfairly treats those who are seen as different. Recalling times when grocery store cashiers were rude to her mother after not understanding her accented English, Natalia remembers asking, "Why are people so mean?" Her mother warned, "When you're Latina, and you're a woman, you gotta fight. It's not gonna be easy, Natalia." In response to these anxiety-inducing incidents as a child, Natalia would "always try to be nice because I knew what Mom went through" and acted as the "helper" and "translator" for new students at her elementary school whenever possible.

This desire to be nice and helpful would transfer to become part of Natalia's purpose for teaching, but it was augmented by her politicization in college. Her educational experience and political awakening at Wesleyan were transformative as she "realized students and children are agents of change." Although she believed that her teachers were supportive of her throughout grade school, she felt that what she learned in college she "should have learned in high school or even before then." Thus, Natalia's purpose for teaching became not just to help students to be nice but also to construct learning experiences that push students to reflect upon and realize their power as agents of change.

While Rosie was the only one to explicitly state that she "came to teaching through wanting to be an activist," her statement holds true for the others as well. Collectively, teacher activists draw their purposes from deeply personal experiences that render a political consciousness about their role as teachers being tied to effecting change. These personal experiences invariably stem from moments of apprehension, when there is an anxious recognition that the world is not as it should be, but instead is unsafe and unjust for too many of us. Anzaldúa (2012) talks about "la facultad" as "the capacity to see in surface phenomena the meaning of deeper realities" (p. 60) and argues that those who are pushed aside and experience oppression are more likely to become sensitized and develop la facultad. It is no mere coincidence, then, that the moments of anxious apprehension, as the portraits in this book illustrate, occur due to the protagonists' identification with positions that are routinely pushed aside: woman, queer, person of color, immigrant, mother. In becoming teacher activists these moments of apprehension—when the protagonists recognize a contradiction between dominant worldviews and their lived experience—provide a foundation for individuals' deeper understanding and grasp of reality that I call critical apprehension. As Collins (2009) points out, seeing contradictions "opens them up for demystification" (p. 109). Pedagogically, teacher activists, after having developed their own critical apprehension of reality, then strive to take action based on these understandings.

Andrews (1991) and Mansbridge (2001) argued that, by itself, consciousness is not enough to motivate action and that here must be more at play for people to act. One interpretation of the protagonists' moments of apprehension is that they represent "moral shocks" (Jasper, 1997), "moral discoveries" (Teske, 1997), or "seminal experiences" (Warren, 2010) when one recognizes a reality dissonant from her core sense of justice, leading to a "sense of outrage" (Jasper, 1997, p. 106) and "righteous anger" (Warren, 2010, p. 27). The moral sentiment of these moments of apprehension makes them stand out: Rosie's innermost sense of who she could love was put into question; Kari and her family served as historical witnesses to how dominant systems treat groups of people unfairly on the basis of their racial identities; Lisa watched as children's eagerness to learn was stripped away by a failing school system; and Natalia realized that she and others need not be trapped by their social location if they are empowered to become agents of change. In each case, moving from anxious to critical apprehension resulted in a motivating passion for teacher activism—an angry apprehension.

The portraits shed light on the subtle and explicit ways critical apprehension stokes the flames of angry apprehension to fuel the pedagogy of teacher activism. Subtly, it was embedded in the urgent strides Lisa made across the roomful of parents at the CEC meeting to grab the microphone and talk passionately about how high-stakes tests are "deforming public education." Kari betrayed her agitation when she rolled her eyes and raised her voice in recalling her graduate school experiences arguing with classmates and professors in an effort to push back against the Model Minority Myth. Even before she was a teacher, Rosie's indignation was obvious in her angry response to her manager at Barnes & Noble when he requested that she and her other low-wage colleagues, instead of the corporation, pitch in for holiday bonuses for custodial staff. Natalia does not shy away from vocal and, sometimes, argumentative rebuttals of her mother or her students when they express discriminatory views.

Explicitly, each teacher activist's purpose-driven action is an expression of angry apprehension. Teacher activists draw critically upon what Rogers

(1990) identified as "cold anger" in her study of community organizing, which "seethes at the injustices of life…rooted in direct experience" (p. 9–10). Orga-nizers help people "take the hot impulse of their anger and cool it down so it can become a useful tool to improve individual lives and the quality of the common community" (Rogers, 1990, p. 10). Rosie's angry apprehension moves her to create safe and activist space for students and teachers because of her own experiences of being marginalized in mainstream spaces. Natalia's realization of her purpose to build consciousness and community with her students reflects her critical apprehension of what she did not receive as a high school student. Kari's commitment to teaching math as a vehicle for social change is a reaction to the unjust conditions of her high school and student teaching math class placements. Finally, Lisa is committed to building solidarity with parents precisely because of the injustice and frustration she experienced as a parent herself.

In each of these cases, the teacher activists' apprehensions motivate action to redress injustices they see before them in schools and communities, which also reflect injustices they have personally experienced in their lives. The com-bined effect of anxious, critical, and angry apprehension is a more self-defined purpose for teaching. In researching Black feminist thought, Collins (2009) asserted the importance of self-definition for people who are placed in constant negotiation between externally constructed images of who they are and how they see themselves. The personal nature of this work makes the pedagogy of teacher activism an "engaged pedagogy" through which teacher activists are "committed to a process of self-actualization that promotes their own well-be-ing" as a precursor to "teach in a manner that empowers students" (hooks, 1994, p. 15). It is their personal indignation and sense of outrage—their angry appre-hension—that fuel their drive toward action and further blur the lines between personal, political, and professional; public and private. This agency is what ful-fills their purpose, which is the topic I will explore next through an examination of how the pedagogy of teacher activism engages with power.

Power: Lessons of Agency

Anzaldúa's (2012) work was derived from her lived experience en la Fron-tera—in the Borderland—which she invoked as both a geographic location along the southwest border between the United States and Mexico and meta-phor for anyone living between, among, and within different cultural contexts.

Those living through the oppression of dominant society's rejection of their intersectional realities are forced to decide how to act in response to their various forms of apprehension. Just as the anxiety of living in a Borderland "is what makes poets write and artists create" (Anzaldúa, 2012, p. 95), it is what makes teachers teach and activists act. Giroux (2001) articulated an important role for educators "to produce, reinvent, and create the ideological and material tools they need to break through the myths and structures that prevent them from transforming an oppressive social reality" (p. 226). In their own words, each protagonist's purpose relates to figuring out ways to transform the "oppressive social reality." For example, Kari refers to the "unfair" system she seeks to challenge and Natalia talks about preparing students for "changing the course of history." More specifically, to fulfill their purpose, teacher activists confront oppression by disrupting the prevailing patterns of power and privilege. The pedagogy of teacher activism shifts power relations through three forms of agency: creative, resistive, and relational.

Rosie and Kari offer differing approaches to challenging dominant structures. Rosie seeks to create space, new structures within which people can identify power and realize their own power. Kari, on the other hand, works more intently to resist dominant structures by "playing the game" in an attempt to disrupt their oppressive nature. However, both of these approaches support the fulfillment of their respective purposes.

Rosie's negative experience in grade school stands in contrast with her more positive experience in college. Feeling as if people were denying the existence of her queer identity, many of her negative experiences in childhood stemmed from her struggle to be fully seen or to have any power at all. In college, when she was out as gay and when she became more of an activist on campus, she was also able to assert herself academically. She felt she had agency. She also had the support of a Lesbian, Gay, Bisexual, Trans and Queer (LGBTQ) student community. Rosie's teaching efforts, then, create alternative environments designed to help students see and understand the experiences of marginalized groups in U.S. history and society, recognize their own realities and agency, and challenge the structures that oppress them.

The gender identity lesson that introduces Rosie's portrait was as much about teaching students social justice content as it was about establishing her classroom as a safe space for nonconforming gender identities. Her introduction of such content into the classroom transformed the space from one where the dominant he/she gender binary would typically be upheld to one where transgender identity was normalized. In a different classroom scene, when she connected the *Grapes of Wrath* to present-day farm workers' struggles for a fair wage, Rosie's students took real-life action by signing onto a petition supporting tomato farm workers in Florida. In her words, students got to "really understand what it's like to run a campaign," thus transforming her classroom into an activist space. In each of these instances, Rosie's approach to shifting power relations is through creative agency. She seeks to structure and create spaces within which students can understand and renegotiate their own relationship to power.

There is no less intentional purpose for how Kari understands her work as part of a struggle to disrupt power relations. When it comes to Kari's challenge to the powerful norms of schooling that often prevent low-income students of color from accessing high-level math courses, her tactics are more reflective of the Capoeira she trains in so diligently.

An Afro-Brazilian martial art disguised in the cloak of ritual dance, the historical practice of Capoeira was a form of resistance to slavery hiding in plain sight, an apt metaphor for Kari's teacher activism. On the one hand, Kari's math teaching can be read traditionally as what any good math teacher would do: she works to cultivate high-level math students. However, when informed by pedagogy concerned with shifting power relations, the teaching of math takes on resistive agency. The confidence and skill Kari's students display in AP Calculus is an attack against the powerful norms that would otherwise see them confined to lower-level classes. Instead of replicating the cycle of oppression that Kari witnessed in her own San Jose high school and while teaching at Berkeley, her teaching activism takes a resistive stand by refusing to succumb to it.

Even obstacles such as students' lack of success with algebra do not prevent Kari from providing access to the power of calculus. Just like capoeiristas in a roda, all students are welcome to participate in Kari's math classroom regardless of perceived ability or skill level. Kari plays the system's game by teaching math but does so through a subtle disruption of the rules. Teacher activists need to navigate between the varied strategies available to them when it comes to challenging dominant structures. At times, they may wish to challenge power openly and create new structures, but they may also choose a more resistant approach that subverts current structures in the interests of those who are typically excluded.

Teacher activists also turn to the promise of relational agency—the proactive cultivation of relationships—to build power with others in order to fulfill their teacher activist purpose. The act of building power *with* as opposed to *over* others is known as relational power (Loomer, 1976; Kreisberg, 1992). Those seeking to build relational power understand, as feminist theorists point out, that personal experiences of mutuality can teach alternatives to power as a form of domination and the importance of seeing social relationships as political articulations (Bloome & Gonzalez in Kreisberg, 1992; Casey, 1993; Sattler, 1997; Weiler, 1988). Teacher activists are uniquely positioned to seek mutual experiences and relationships with those they are closest to in their professional roles: students, parents, and other educators and activists. Lisa seeks opportunities to build solidarity with parents whenever she can. And, for Natalia, relationships serve as the cornerstone for consciousness raising and community-building efforts with both students and educators.

Lisa's purpose of improving schools by working together with teachers and parents breaks down the typical barriers erected between these two groups. In urban school settings, the teacher-parent relationship is mitigated by the relative power teachers generally have over parents. Lisa's experience as a parent emphasized this power relationship when she was uncomfortable being out as gay with her son's grade school teachers. She remembers the feeling of "coming as an 'other' into the school system and not feeling supported," which helps explain why, as a teacher activist, Lisa seeks out ways to partner with parent activists.

Lisa's teacher activism is notable for her focus on proactively seeking to build relationships with parents. Her work with CEJ and Lisa's commitment to giving up Saturday mornings for her local CEC meetings are attempts to build relational power as a teacher in these parent- and community-led activist spaces. Even in her work with the teacher-dominated GEM, she appeals to her teacher activist colleagues by stressing that the "key" to their success will be "an alliance between parents and teachers." Teacher activists who focus solely on their classroom pedagogy or their work organizing with other teachers to fight for educational justice fall short of Lisa's call to forge alliances with parents and communities.

Natalia's approach to teacher activism—both inside and outside of her classroom—utilizes relational agency significantly. Her deep attention to her everyday interactions with students and colleagues is central to her efforts to shift power relations. As a young girl, Natalia was concerned about her relationships with others, seeking to build caring connections with her peers in elementary school. Her emphasis on recognizing and seeing others fully is borne out by her daily classroom handshaking routine. The communal atmosphere she works to cultivate at New York Collective of Radical Educators (NYCoRE) members meetings and then, more specifically, for members of color, and the hugs, kisses, smiles, and squeals when she is with the Venceremos Brigade all represent the central necessity of human fellowship when it comes to working for change.

Natalia does not push her students to become leaders and agents of change without forging family-like bonds. When Natalia challenged the use of homophobic language by some of her Young Leadership Board (YLB) members, there was tension between the students and Natalia. She was wrought with emotion and felt like her "family was breaking up." However, because her students felt just as strongly, also describing YLB "like a family," they were able to work through tensions together because they have created "a little space where they all feel comfortable talking to each other and being honest with each other." Her proactive cultivation of relationships enables Natalia to challenge her students, expand their political consciousness, and dare them to be leaders.

Teacher activist agencies move us away from vague or clichéd notions of what it means to be change agents and answer Darder's (2011) call for a "pedagogy of the body" in order to "free students and teachers from educational and social constraints that repress the development of voice, disrupt democratic participation, and thwart self-determination" (p. 351). Very specifically, creative agency supports space within which marginalized people's voice can be developed. Resistive agency provides tools for presence and self-determination in spaces that are normally exclusionary. Relational agency enables the full participation of teachers, students, and parents in the educational process. However, whether acting in ways that are creative, resistive, or relational to fulfill purpose, one final element is necessary to sustain the pedagogy of teacher activism: a sense of hope and possibility.

Possibility: Lessons of Hope

Anyone who has ever taught understands how demanding the job is. For all the hours spent in schools teaching, there are at least half as many spent outside of the regular school day when teachers give extra help to students, plan lessons, grade student work, attend professional development sessions, talk to parents, and more. At times, the demands of teaching on top of the commitments that people have in their everyday lives seem impossible. Teacher activists add to their long list of responsibilities all of the activist work they do outside of their classrooms. Such overwhelming commitments beg the question of what sustains them. The answer that I will offer here is that teacher activists are sustained by a sense of hope and possibility for change.

All of the participants in this study face the difficulty of balancing their time and energy across their teaching, activism, and personal lives. Rosie's expressions of exasperation toward the end of her portrait were from feeling "bogged down" and like she "just can't keep up" with all that she has to do as a teacher activist. The balance of spending time visiting her family in New Jersey on the weekends or spending time with her partner and the time it takes to attend multiple meetings and actions as well as teaching can be overwhelming.

Natalia attempts to regiment her schedule to accommodate her teaching and activist commitments. Amid a busy weekly schedule of various activities that include everything from school responsibilities to therapy, she assigns Thursdays to activist meetings. She feels guilty when she tells people that she cannot make it to a protest or important meeting because "I actually have to grade and I have to plan."

Kari shares feelings of guilt over how much time she dedicates to training Capoeira, which has taken her away from activist work outside of school. Yet, somehow she still maintains her commitment as a lead organizer for the Creating Balance conference. And, I rarely meet up with Lisa when she is not either coming or going to a meeting, conference, action, or some activist-related event. Their lives are fast paced and overflowing. It is a wonder that they can all keep up and above water.

If purpose brings teacher activists to their work in the first place, which they fulfill via actions to disrupt power relations, then it is their sense of hope and possibility that sustains their power and energy, even when their work might seem too much. Duncan-Andrade (2009) argued that educators must nurture "critical hope" in students who face the harsh challenges that exist for low-income, urban communities of color. Borrowing heavily from this concept, I argue that critical hope is just as important for teacher activists as it is for students, maintaining their sense of possibility and helping them persevere in their work. They engage in a "humanizing pedagogy", which requires a critical sociohistorical analysis and understanding (or apprehension) of the educational context and the development of pedagogical approaches that speak to the "day-to-day reality, struggles, concerns, and dreams" of their students (Bartolomé, 1994, p. 176). I will trace how the three elements—material, Socratic, and audacious—constituting critical hope manifest in the work of the teacher activists.

Material hope helps people gain a sense of control over the forces that affect their lives. For teachers, one of the most significant resources they can offer to nurture students' material hope is quality teaching that builds students' academic skills (Duncan-Andrade, 2009). While all four protagonists show evidence of quality teaching in their portraits, Kari's example is perhaps the most illustrative of this element of critical hope.

Kari's unwillingness to compromise the integrity of her rigorous math instruction is a testament to her commitment to ensuring that her students develop the material resources that higher-level math skills will provide. When she arrived at her high school, seniors were graduating by doing math PBAs demonstrating ninth- and tenth-grade math skills. Resulting from years of dedicated improvement on the part of the entire math department, seniors now demonstrate knowledge of calculus in their math PBAs. Importantly, this marked improvement has not been made while ignoring students' social and emotional needs.

Material hope extends beyond the academic classroom and helps students and teachers "connect schooling to the real, *material* conditions of urban life" (Duncan-Andrade, 2009, p. 187). It is not surprising, then, that Kari credits much of her students' academic success to the relationships they build and the attention given to student needs through her school's advisory structure. In advisory, students are supported to navigate life realities like peer pressure, dating, bullying, and tragedy. They are not asked to divorce these conditions of their real lives from their school experience. The attention Kari gives to both academic instruction and the material conditions in her students' lives is what provides the material hope for gaining a sense of control over the forces affecting their lives. Material hope also helps Kari see and understand markers of real progress and possibility as a teacher activist. Each year her students learn more complex math skills and each year she helps students graduate and move into postsecondary education. She sees possibility for the world in her students. "They're the ones who need to be heard; they're the ones who create change. I just think that they have so much more potential than I do," Kari says. The material hope that Kari provides contributes to that potential.

Socratic hope stems from the reflective examination of the difficulty and painfulness of everyday life and the recognition that shared struggle is part of the path toward the realization of justice (Duncan-Andrade, 2009). I have already established how the protagonists' biographical struggles lead to critical apprehension, which stresses the importance of personal reflection for understanding how to fight for a better world. In Natalia's case, reflection upon her own struggles and education as a Latina in the New York City public schools has led her to employ an activist pedagogy that humanizes her students as agents of change. Her work to see and recognize her students, as well as helping them see and recognize each other, builds bonds that enable them to reflect with each other and act together. The aforementioned example of Natalia's decision to challenge YLB student leaders to confront and deal with their homophobia is a prime example of employing Socratic hope. More importantly, the fact that student leaders took initiative to resolve tensions on their own helps Natalia understand the possibility embedded in her work. "Those are the moments where I'm, like, this is beautiful," Natalia reflected about the YLB's resolution of tensions among the members. Those are also the moments that will keep Natalia coming back to her work committed to the relational agency that opened doors to the possibility displayed by the YLB.

Rosie's work is similar in that it has stemmed from her experience of pain and marginalization as a student. She strives to create classroom spaces within which students can examine who they are and what power they can have when they critically examine the world around them. Thus, it is important for teacher activists to take stock of their personal struggles and how they have faced pain or suffering. Such reflection does not only help them develop pedagogical purpose but also enables them to build an empathic solidarity with students and a Socratic hope that fuels their work. In Rosie's case, Socratic hope can be found at the end of her portrait when her students are proudly presenting their radio journalism projects. These projects, a result of the creative space Rosie helped to build, all positioned students as change agents, critical of, yet hopeful for their everyday realities. Rosie's beaming smile during the student presentations is all one needs to see to know that these moments provide sustenance to her creative agency.

Finally, audacious hope lies in one's willingness to stare down the painful path and, "despite the overwhelming odds against us making it down that path to change, [...] make the journey again and again" (Duncan-Andrade, 2009, p. 191). Lisa's perseverance over time as a veteran teacher is a testament to her audacity to hope. The vision she lays out for the solidarity, she seeks between teachers and parents, is audacious in its expansiveness. She knows that it seems a far-flung dream to think that tens of thousands of teachers and parents will come together to shut down midtown Manhattan demanding better public schools, but that does not stop her from continuing her teacher activism in pursuit of this possibility.

As a child, Lisa saw hope in the possibility of the Civil Rights Movement and thought it silly that her father assured her that there would be plenty of just causes for her to work on when she grew older. Sure enough, there is a seemingly endless list of educational injustices facing teachers and parents for Lisa to work on. Yet, however overwhelming I found the laundry list of issues when they were raised at various meetings I attended with Lisa, it is not something in which Lisa finds despair. Instead, she seeks possibility, constantly searching for the issue or moment that will help bring teachers, parents, and communities together. The closing scene of Lisa's portrait is one of audacious hope. That in one teacher Lisa can see 100,000 and in 20–30 parents she envisions 20,000–30,000 is emblematic of the audaciousness that sustains her teacher activism. She has embarked upon many journeys for justice, as a labor activist, antiwar demonstrator, parent activist, and teacher activist. There is no sign that she or other teacher activists will cease their travels any time soon in the hopeful search for change.

Conclusion

Thus far, the pedagogy of teacher activism has laid out how purpose derived from apprehension is fulfilled by powerful forms of agency and sustained through a steady hopefulness in the possibility of a just society. What brings the pedagogy of teacher activism full circle is the way in which possibility and hope continuously revive and renew teacher activists' purpose and commitment. Like Rosie reflects at the end of her portrait, "the best part about being a teacher is that every year you get to start off new." Freire (in Darder, 2011) stressed the "capacity to always begin anew" as an "indispensible quality of a good teacher" (p. 188). The opportunity for renewal is important and powerful. It reconnects the pedagogy of teacher activism to the procreative project of teaching and serves as a reminder that teaching is an act of creation stemming from the uneasy apprehension that things are not as they should be. Each school year offers a renewed sense of purpose that can feed teacher activist agency toward shifting power relations with a refreshed hopefulness at the possibility of change. The cyclical nature of schooling and teaching lends itself to the pedagogy of teacher activism, which is fluid and dynamic.

Sadly, in recent years mainstream education reform has underscored an increasingly technical focus on teaching and learning that ignores the fluidity and dynamism that the pedagogy for teacher activism relies upon. Even as reformers claim they carry the mantle of civil rights and social justice, there has been an increased emphasis on the mechanistic use of student test scores for determining everything from graduation and promotion, to school closures, to teacher evaluation ratings. Additionally, current popular refrains in the mainstream education reform movement have articulated a purpose of education that has trouble extending beyond the training of a 21st-century work force, which curiously omits the need to focus on the cultivation of a healthy democratic society. As this book is being published, the United States is in the midst of a presidential election cycle that features major cracks and fissures in the country's democratic fabric. Candidates and campaigns thrive as they prop themselves up with vile characterizations of people of color, women, queer people, and people living in poverty. Whether such political tactics result in electoral victory, it is clear that we need a serious recalibration of our social and democratic scales.

I do not deny that students should be learning academic skills, which may very well translate to proficiency on standardized tests. So, too, should they be adequately prepared with the job skills necessary for employment in fast-paced and swiftly changing job markets. However, so long as visions of educational purpose are focused on male-dominated capitalistic politics of production, they will fail to offer young people, teachers, or society a deeper and more meaningful purpose for education. When teaching is understood as a purely technical enterprise aimed at improved test scores and workforce development, then the deeply personal and political nature of teaching and education is misunderstood. The pedagogies stemming from such a misunderstanding will not be transformative, engaged, creative, critical, or humanizing. More students testing well and becoming ready-made workers for an economy that continues to further concentrate wealth and resources in the hands of the very few will not shift the unequal power relations that govern our society. Prevailing pedagogies that align with the current reforms lack the imagination for what might be possible if we pursue education for freedom, justice, and liberation.

Teacher activists offer an alternative to the tide of reform that has left so many educators, students, families, and communities dissatisfied in its wake. It is important for our field to support and follow the lead of teacher activists and teacher activist groups, who on a daily basis are employing and innovating the pedagogy of teacher activism, centered on a womanist politics of creation. Teacher educators must examine coursework and field experiences to identify ways in which they can support the cultivation of purpose, power, and possibility in the teaching candidates in their programs. Teacher unions should bolster their commitment to building solidarity with youth and community organizations fighting for a just society, and specifically support teacher activism and leadership within their ranks. Education researchers must ensure that we are supporting scholarship and training scholars to resist the temptation to boil teaching and learning down to a technical science and instead engage questions that explore the complex fluidity of the social, political, and cultural world of education. Similarly, reformers should take heed of the pedagogy of teacher activism to reimagine what teaching is and can be and usher in policies that will support teachers to develop their sense of purpose, power, and possibility. To teach with purpose and passion, which stem from the very core of one's being, is to fulfill the promise of education as a human endeavor for freedom. The education that results from such teaching should give us hope for the creation of a world where power is shared for the uplift of those who have been held down in the past and for the possibility of teaching that can truly change the world.

References

Andrews, M. (1991). *Lifetimes of commitment: Aging, politics, psychology.* Cambridge, UK: Cambridge University Press.

Anzaldúa, G. (2012). *Borderlands/la frontera: The new Mestiza* (4th ed.). San Francisco: Aunt Lute Books.

Bartolomé, L.I. (1994). Beyond the methods fetish: Toward a humanizing pedagogy. *Harvard Educational Review,* 64(2), 173–195.

Casey, K. (1993). *I answer with my life: Life histories of women teachers working for social change.* New York: Routledge.

Collins, P.H. (2009). *Black feminist thought: Knowledge, consciousness, and the politics of empowerment.* New York: Routledge Classics.

Darder, A. (2011). *A dissident voice: Essays on culture, pedagogy, and power.* New York: Peter Lang.

Duncan-Andrade, J.M.R. (2009). Note to educators: Hope required when growing roses in concrete. *Harvard Educational Review,* 79(2), 181–194.

Giroux, H.A. (1992). *Border crossings: Cultural workers and the politics of education.* New York: Routledge.

Giroux, H.A. (2001). *Theory and resistance in education: Towards a pedagogy for the opposition.* Westport, CT: Bergin & Garvey.

Giroux, H.A. (2007). Introduction: Democracy, education, and the politics of critical pedagogy. In P. McLaren & J.L. Kincheloe (eds.), *Critical pedagogy: Where are we now?* (pp. 1–5). New York: Peter Lang.

Grumet, M. (1988). *Bitter milk: Women and teaching.* Amherst, MA: University of Massachusetts Press.

Hermance, M. (2012). From the word to the world: Freire's concept of 'becoming.' *UCLA Graduate School of Education and Information Studies Social Sciences and Comparative Education Newsletter,* 3(3), 2.

hooks, b. (1994). *Teaching to transgress: Education as the practice of freedom.* New York: Routledge.

Jasper, J.M. (1997). *The art of moral protest: Culture, biography, and creativity in social movements.* Chicago: University of Chicago Press.

Kreisberg, S. (1992). *Transforming power: Domination, empowerment, and education.* Albany, NY: SUNY Press.

Loomer, B. (1976). Two conceptions of power. *Criterion,* 15(1), 11–29.

Mansbridge, J.J. (2001). The making of oppositional consciousness. In J.J. Mansbridge & A. Morris (eds.), *Oppositional consciousness: The subjective roots of social protest* (pp. 1–19). Chicago: University of Chicago Press.

Oxford Dictionaries. (n.d.). Definition of apprehension in English. Retrieved June 10, 2016, from http://www.oxforddictionaries.com.revproxy.brown.edu/definition/english/apprehension

Rogers, M.B. (1990). *Cold anger: A story of faith and power politics.* Denton, TX: University of North Texas Press.

Sattler, C.L. (1997). *Talking about a revolution: The politics and practice of feminist teaching.* Cresskill, NJ: Hampton Press, Inc.

Simmons, W. (2013, April 9). *The Annenberg Institute at 20: Executive director Warren Simmons looks back at two decades of school reform.* Retrieved January 8, 2014, from http://annenberginstitute.org/commentary/2013/04/annenberg-institute-20-executive-director-warren-simmons-looks-back-two-decades-s

Warren, M.R. (2010). *Fire in the heart: How white activists embrace racial justice.* New York: Oxford University Press.

Weiler, K. (1988). *Women teaching for change: Gender, Class & Power.* Westport, CT: Bergin & Garvey.

REFERENCES

Adams, M., Bell, L.A., & Griffin. P. (eds.). (1997). *Teaching for diversity and social justice: A sourcebook*. New York: Routledge.

Andrews, M. (1991). *Lifetimes of commitment: Aging, politics, psychology*. Cambridge, UK: Cambridge University Press.

Anyon, J. (1980). Social class and the hidden curriculum of work. *Journal of Education, 162*(1), 67–92.

Anyon, J. (2005). *Radical possibilities: Public policy, urban education, and a new social movement*. New York: Routledge.

Anzaldúa, G. (2012). *Borderlands/la frontera: The new Mestiza* (4th ed.). San Francisco: Aunt Lute Books.

Apple, M. (1982). *Education and power*. London: Routledge & Kegan Paul.

Au, W., Bigelow, B., Burant, T., & Salas, K.D. (2005). Teacher organizers take quality into their own hands. *Rethinking Schools*. Retrieved May 13, 2007 from http://www.rethinkingschools.org/archive/20_02/orga202.shtml

Ayers, W. (1998). Popular education: Teaching for social justice. In W. Ayers, J.A. Hunt & T. Quinn (eds.), *Teaching for social justice* (pp. xvii–xxv). New York: The New Press and Teachers College Press.

Bartolomé, L.I. (1994). Beyond the methods fetish: Toward a humanizing pedagogy. *Harvard Educational Review, 64*(2), 173–195.

Bernstein, B. (1975). *Class, codes, and control*. London: Routledge and Kegan Paul.

Bourdieu, P. & Passeron, J.C. (1977). *Reproduction in education, society and culture*. London: Sage Publications.

Bowles, S. & Gintis, H. (1977). *Schooling in capitalist America: Educational reform and the contradictions of economic life*. New York: Basic Books.

Bryant, J. (2015, September 18). Seattle teachers' strike a win for social justice. Retrieved June 16, 2016, from https://ourfuture.org/20150918/seattle-teachers-strike-a-win-for-social-justice

Casey, K. (1993). *I answer with my life: Life histories of women teachers working for social change*. New York: Routledge.

Catone, K. (2013). Teachers unions as partners, not as adversaries. *Voices in Urban Education, 36*, 52–58.

Catone, K.C., Mangual Figueroa, A., & Picower, B. (2010, May). *The beautiful struggle: Teacher activism as professional development*. Paper presented at the Annual Meeting of the American Education Research Association, Denver, CO.

Chicago Teachers Union. (2012). As Chicago teachers strike enters fourth day, a new poll proves majority of parents and taxpayers approve of fair contract fight. Retrieved September 15, 2012, from http://www.ctunet.com/blog/new-poll-shows-that-that-majority-of-the-public-supports-the-strike

Collins, P.H. (2009). *Black feminist thought: Knowledge, consciousness, and the politics of empowerment*. New York: Routledge Classics.

Cooper, A. J. (1988). *A voice from the south*. New York: Oxford University Press.

Darder, A. (2011). *A dissident voice: Essays on culture, pedagogy, and power*. New York: Peter Lang.

Delpit, L. (1995). *Other people's children: Cultural conflict in the classroom*. New York: The New Press.

Doster, A. (2008, February 25). The conscious classroom: A new generation of educators, frustrated with ineffective reforms, turns to pedagogy focused on social justice. *The Nation*. Retrieved October 22, 2012, from http://www.thenation.com/article/conscious-classroom

Duncan-Andrade, J.M.R. (2009). Note to educators: Hope required when growing roses in concrete. *Harvard Educational Review, 79*(2), 181–194.

Duncan-Andrade, J.M.R. & Morrell, E. (2008). *The art of critical pedagogy: Possibilities for moving from theory to practice in urban schools*. New York: Peter Lang.

Freire, P. (1993). *Pedagogy of the oppressed*. New York: Continuum.

Gilmore, R.W. (2007). *Golden gulag: Prisons, surplus, crisis, and opposition in globalizing California*. Berkeley, CA: University of California Press.

Giroux, H.A. (1992). *Border crossings: Cultural workers and the politics of education*. New York: Routledge.

Giroux, H.A. (2001). *Theory and resistance in education: Towards a pedagogy for the opposition*. Westport, CT: Bergin & Garvey.

Giroux, H.A. (2007). Introduction: Democracy, education, and the politics of critical pedagogy. In P. McLaren & J.L. Kincheloe (eds.), *Critical pedagogy: Where are we now?* (pp. 1–5). New York: Peter Lang.

Giroux, H.A. & McLaren, P. (1986). Teacher education and the politics of engagement: The case for democratic schooling. *Harvard Educational Review, 56*(3), 213–238.

Gordon, J.A. (2001). Why they couldn't wait: A critique of the Black-Jewish conflict over community control in Ocean Hill-Brownsville (1967–1971). New York: Routledge Falmer.

Gothamist. (2005). Hot 97 is in hot water. Retrieved July 17, 2012, from http://gothamist. com/2005/01/24/hot_97_in_hot_water.php

Grassroots Education Movement (GEM) NYC. (n.d.). About us. Retrieved October 22, 2012, from http://gemnyc.org/about

Grumet, M. (1988). Bitter milk: Women and teaching. Amherst, MA: University of Massachusetts Press.

Heath, S.B. (1983). Ways with words. Cambridge, UK: Cambridge University Press.

Hermance, M. (2012). From the word to the world: Freire's concept of 'becoming.' UCLA Graduate School of Education and Information Studies Social Sciences and Comparative Education Newsletter, 3(3), 2.

Hoffer, E. (1951). The true believer. New York: Harper & Row.

Hoo, S.S. (2004). We change the world by doing nothing. Teacher Education Quarterly, 39(1), 199–211.

hooks, b. (1994). Teaching to transgress: Education as the practice of freedom. New York: Routledge.

Hunt, J.A. (1998). Of stories, seeds and the promises of social justice. In W. Ayers, J.A. Hunt & T. Quinn (eds.), Teaching for social justice (pp. xiii–xv). New York: The New Press and Teachers College Press.

Jasper, J.M. (1997). The art of moral protest: Culture, biography, and creativity in social movements. Chicago: University of Chicago Press.

Johnson, L. (2002). "Making democracy real": Teacher union and community activism to promote diversity in the NewYork City public schools, 1935–1950. Urban Education, 37(5). 566–587.

Kreisberg, S. (1992). Transforming power: Domination, empowerment, and education. Albany, NY: SUNY Press.

Kumashiro, K.K. (2012). Bad teacher: How blaming teachers distorts the bigger picture. New York: Teachers College Press.

Lawrence-Lightfoot, S. & Davis, J.H. (1997). The art and science of portraiture. San Francisco: Jossey-Bass.

Levine, D. (2002). The Milwaukee platoon school battle: Lessons for activist teachers. The Urban Review, 34(1), 47–69.

Lipman, P. (2011). The new political economy of urban education: Neoliberalism, race, and the right to the city. New York: Routledge.

Loomer, B. (1976). Two conceptions of power. Criterion, 15(1), 11–29.

Lorde, A. (1984). The master's tools will never dismantle the master's house. In A. Lorde, Sister outsider: Essays and speeches by Audre Lorde (pp. 110–113). Berkeley, CA: Crossing Press.

MacLeod, J. (1995). Ain't no makin' it: Aspirations and attainment in a low-income neighborhood. Boulder, CO: Westview Press.

Mansbridge, J.J. (2001). The making of oppositional consciousness. In J.J. Mansbridge & A. Morris (eds.), Oppositional consciousness: The subjective roots of social protest (pp. 1–19). Chicago: University of Chicago Press.

Marshall, C. & Anderson, A.L. (eds.). (2009). *Activist educators: Breaking past limits*. New York: Routledge.

Marx, K. & Engels, F. (1848). *Manifesto of the Communist party*. In R.C. Tucker (ed.), *The Marx-Engels Reader* (2nd ed.) (pp. 473–500). New York: W.W. Norton & Company.

McAdam, D. & Paulsen, R. (1993). Specifying the relationship between social ties and activism. *American Journal of Sociology*, 99(3), 640–667.

McAlister, S. & Catone, K.C. (2013). Real parent power: Relational organizing for sustainable school reform. *National Civic Review*, 102(1), 26–32.

McLaren, P. (2007). *Life in schools: An introduction to critical pedagogy in the foundations of education* (5th ed.). Boston: Pearson Allyn and Bacon.

MetLife, Inc. (2013). *The MetLife survey of the American teacher: Challenges for school leadership*. New York: MetLife Foundation. Retrieved March 23, 2013, from https://www.metlife.com/metlife-foundation/about/survey-american-teacher.html?WT.mc_id=vu1101

Moe, T. (1980). *The organization of interests: Incentives and the internal dynamics of political interest groups*. Chicago: University of Chicago Press.

Montaño, T., López-Torres, L., DeLissovoy, N., Pacheco, M., & Stillman, J. (2002). Teachers as activists: Teacher development and alternate sites of learning. *Equity & Excellence in Education*, 35(3), 265–275.

Morgan, R. (ed.). (1970). *Sisterhood is powerful: An anthology of writings from the women's liberation movement*. New York: Random House.

Oakes, J. & Lipton, M. (1999). *Teaching to Change the World*. Boston: McGraw-Hill College.

Oakes, J. & Rogers J. (2006). *Learning power: Organizing for education and justice*. New York: Teachers College Press.

Oxford Dictionaries. (n.d.). Definition of apprehension in English. Retrieved June 10, 2016, from http://www.oxforddictionaries.com.revproxy.brown.edu/definition/english/apprehension

Payne, C.M. (2008). Introduction. In C.M. Payne & C.S. Strickland (eds.), *Teach freedom: Education for liberation in the African-American tradition* (pp. 1–11). New York: Teachers College Press.

Perrillo, J. (2012). *Uncivil rights: Teachers, unions, and race in the battle for school equity*. Chicago: The University of Chicago Press.

Perry, T., Moses, R.P., Wynne, J.T., Cortes Jr., E. & Delpit, L. (eds.). (2010). *Quality education as a constitutional right: Creating a grassroots movement to transform public schools*. Boston: Beacon Press.

Peterson, B. (1999). Survival and justice: Rethinking teacher union strategy. In B. Peterson & M. Charney (eds.), *Transforming teacher unions: Fighting for better schools and social justice* (pp. 11–19). Milwaukee, WI: Rethinking Schools.

Peterson, B. (2011, September 21). It's time to re-imagine and reinvent the MTEA. Speech presented at Milwaukee Teachers Education Association Convocation, Milwaukee, WI. Retrieved September 3, 2013, from www.mtea.org/Public/pdf/Re-imaginespeech.pdf

Peterson, B. & Charney, M. (eds.). (1999). *Transforming teacher unions: Fighting for better schools and social justice*. Milwaukee, WI: Rethinking Schools.

Picower, B. (2007). Supporting new educators to teach for social justice: The critical inquiry project model. *Penn Perspectives on Urban Education, 5*(1). Retrieved September 15, 2012, from http://www.urbanedjournal.org/node/147

Picower, B. (2012). *Practice what you teach: Social justice education in the classroom and the streets.* New York: Routledge.

Picower, B. (2013). Education should be free! Occupy the DOE!: Teacher activists involved in the Occupy Wall Street movement. *Critical Studies in Education, 54*(1), 44–56.

Rethinking Schools. (2012). New teachers' union movement in the making. *Rethinking Schools, 27*(2), 5–6.

Robinson, C.J. (1983). *Black Marxism: The making of the Black radical tradition.* Chapel Hill, NC: University of North Carolina Press.

Rogers, M.B. (1990). *Cold anger: A story of faith and power politics.* Denton, TX: University of North Texas Press.

Rogers, R., Mosley, M., Kramer, M.A., & the Literacy for Social Justice Teacher Research Group. (2009). *Designing socially just learning communities: Critical literacy education across the lifespan.* New York: Routledge.

Sattler, C.L. (1997). *Talking about a revolution: The politics and practice of feminist teaching.* Cresskill, NJ: Hampton Press, Inc.

Seidman, I. (2006). *Interviewing as qualitative research: A guide for researchers in education and the social sciences.* New York: Teachers College Press.

Simpson, A. (2007). On ethnographic refusal: Indigeneity, 'voice' and colonial citizenship. *Junctures: The Journal for Thematic Dialogue, 9,* 67–80.

Simmons, W. (2013, April 9). *The Annenberg Institute at 20: Executive director Warren Simmons looks back at two decades of school reform.* Retrieved January 8, 2014, from http://annenberg institute.org/commentary/2013/04/annenberg-institute-20-executive-director-warren-simmons-looks-back-two-decades-s

Simmons, W. (2013, May 9). *What do we know about "reformers".* Speech presented at the Learning First Alliance Leadership Council Meeting. Retrieved September 20, 2013, from http://www.learningfirst.org/sites/default/files/assets/Leadership%20Council%20Meeting%202013%20Report.pdf

Sokolower, J. (2012). Lessons in social justice unionism: An interview with Chicago Teachers Union president Karen Lewis. *Rethinking Schools, 27*(2), 10–17.

Stern, S. (2007a, March 19). Radical equations. *City Journal.* Retrieved September 15, 2013, from http://www.city-journal.org/html/eon2007-03-19ss.html

Stern, S. (2007b, May 11). Radical math at the DOE. *City Journal.* Retrieved September 15, 2013, from http://www.city-journal.org/html/eon2007-05-11ss.html

Teaching Tolerance. (1999). A solitary struggle. *Teaching Tolerance, 16.* Retrieved September 15, 2012, from http://www.tolerance.org/magazine/number-16-fall-1999/solitary-struggle

Teske, N. (1997). *Political activists in America: The identity construction model of political participation.* Cambridge, UK: Cambridge University Press.

Urban, W.J. (1989). Teacher activism. In D. Warren (ed.), *American teachers* (pp. 190–209). New York: Macmillan.

Warren, M.R. (2010). *Fire in the heart: How white activists embrace racial justice.* New York: Oxford University Press.

Weiler, K. (1988). *Women teaching for change: Gender, Class & Power.* Westport, CT: Bergin & Garvey.

Willis, P. (1981). *Learning to labor: How working class kids get working class jobs.* New York: Columbia University Press.

Narrative, Dialogue and the Political Production of Meaning

Michael A. Peters
Peter McLaren
Series Editors

To submit a manuscript or proposal for editorial consideration, please contact:

Dr. Peter McLaren
UCLA Los Angeles
School of Education &
Information Studies
Moore Hall 3022C
Los Angeles, CA 90095

Dr. Michael Peters
University of Waikato
P.O. Box 3105
Faculty of Education
Hamilton 3240
New Zealand

WE ARE THE STORIES WE TELL. The book series Education and Struggle focuses on conflict as a discursive process where people struggle for legitimacy and the narrative process becomes a political struggle for meaning. But this series will also include the voices of authors and activists who are involved in conflicts over material necessities in their communities, schools, places of worship, and public squares as part of an ongoing search for dignity, self-determination, and autonomy. This series focuses on conflict and struggle within the realm of educational politics based around a series of interrelated themes: indigenous struggles; Western-Islamic conflicts; globalization and the clash of worldviews; neo-liberalism as the war within; colonization and neocolonization; the coloniality of power and decolonial pedagogy; war and conflict; and the struggle for liberation. It publishes narrative accounts of specific struggles as well as theorizing "conflict narratives" and the political production of meaning in educational studies. During this time of global conflict and the crisis of capitalism, Education and Struggle promises to be on the cutting edge of social, cultural, educational, and political transformation.

Central to the series is the idea that language is a process of social, cultural, and class conflict. The aim is to focus on key semiotic, literary, and political concepts as a basis for a philosophy of language and culture where the underlying materialist philosophy of language and culture serves as the basis for the larger project that we might call dialogism (after Bakhtin's usage). As the late V.N. Volosinov suggests "Without signs there is no ideology," "Everything ideological possesses semiotic value," and "individual consciousness is a socio-ideological fact." It is a small step to claim, therefore, "consciousness itself can arise and become a viable fact only in the material embodiment of signs." This series is a vehicle for materialist semiotics in the narrative and dialogue of education and struggle.

To order other books in this series, please contact our Customer Service Department:

(800) 770-LANG (within the U.S.)
(212) 647-7706 (outside the U.S.)
(212) 647-7707 FAX

Or browse online by series:

www.peterlang.com